The Cocktail Jungle

The Cocktail Jungle

A Girl's Field Guide to Shaking and Stirring

Nicole Beland

RUNNING PRESS
PHILADELPHIA · LONDON

9 8 7 6 5 4 3 2 1

Digit on the right indicates the number of this printing

Library of Congress Cataloging-in-Publication Number 2002093010

ISBN 0-7624-1437-5

Cover and interior illustrations by Amy Saidens, Arts Counsel, Inc.
Cover and interior design by Alicia Freile
Edited by Lynn Rosen
Typography: Clarendon and Univers

This book may be ordered by mail from the publisher.
Please include $2.50 for postage and handling.
But try your bookstore first!

Running Press Book Publishers
125 South Twenty-second Street
Philadelphia, Pennsylvania 19103-4399

Visit us on the web!
www.runningpress.com

Ref
TX
951
.B39
2003

Contents

Welcome to the Cocktail Jungle

The big question isn't whether or not you and your friends want to go out for a cocktail (*of course* you do), it's where. From the Latest Lounge to the Neighborhood Pub, there's a destination out there that can transform your night into whatever you want it to be. Glamorous? Sophisticated? Laid-back? Silly? Exotic? Completely out of control? Don't feel like you have to pick just one, because you can have all of the above, any night of the week. But you probably already know that. If you're like most twenty- and thirty-somethings, heading out for a drink and a chat is hardly an occasional treat—it's a fact of life. It's simply how we hang out. If you think about it, you've probably spent more time in bars over the past two years than your mother has in her entire lifetime. Poor Mom! How did she ever get anything done?

Refreshments aside, bars are where we go to have heart-to-hearts with our oldest friends. They're where we take the people we want to get to know better (male and female). They're where we want to be when we're happy or miserable, jazzed or blah, horny or satisfied. We even end up scoring priceless information—about job openings, travel ideas, apartment rentals, stores, spas, yoga studios, restaurants, concerts—all from people we meet in bars. For our generation, socializing in bars is second nature, and in spite of the fact that men originally dominated watering holes, the girls are just as good at it as the boys. Though guys never did seem to mind the invasion. On the contrary, they've started to follow our lead and are finally ordering all the sweet, colorful concoctions we've been raving about for years. A stud holding a Sour-Apple Martini is no longer a rare sight.

Speaking of Sour-Apple Martinis—at the heart of every bar are its cocktails, and great cocktails are worth going out for in and of themselves. They were invented during Prohibition when bartenders used everything they could find to cover up the nasty taste of illegally made liquor, but, like perfume, the results turned out to be far too good to give up when the initial problem was solved. The creation of cocktails did more than just make liquor yummier, it made it more complicated, more delicate, more interesting—in a word, more feminine. And we women have been sipping them ever since. But now more than ever, bars are filling up with chicks who want to kick back and have something cold and sparkling placed between their manicured fingertips. From the simple to the sublime, we're interested in experimenting with cocktails to find out what we like and what we don't. We're trying them on like clothes and keeping them only if we like them. In the candyland of cocktails, you never, *ever* have to finish your drink.

This book is about more than just bars and drinks, it's about music, men, mingling, and atmosphere. You'll find tips on how to play darts in a dive, request a jazz standard at a piano bar, pick the best tequila to sip straight-up, master punk rock karaoke, break the ice with a stranger, and otherwise have an amazing time every time you go out, wherever you choose to go. And if you happen to get the urge to mix up a batch of cocktails at home or throw your very own bash, you'll find advice on how to do that too. All of these fantastic nightlife options are yours for the taking. So, where do you want to go tonight?

The Neighborhood Pub

Ahhhh . . . the corner bar. It's like a spa for beer-drinkers. Some are even beautiful—old places with intricately carved wooden bars, big windows, smiling bartenders, and a dozen varieties of beer on tap. Others are worn-and-torn dives with duct-tape-covered vinyl booths, ancient pinball machines, heavily scarred bartenders, and nothing but domestic beers in cans. You've got to love both, because they're your warm-and-fuzzy homes away from home—the kinds of places that make you feel like you're one of the gang (or possibly even a member of one).

The local pub tends to be the destination of choice when it's cold and raining and you're not even sure you want to go out. Or when you definitely feel like partying, but only if you can wear jeans and sneakers and leave your MAC products at home. And why should you primp? This is nightlife at its most effortless, so showing up in a pencil skirt and a pair of stilettos will only end up making you feel out of place. It could also get you a little more attention from Mick, the 72-year-old ex-sailor sitting at the end of the bar, than you were looking for (if he lifts up his shirt and offers to make the mermaid tattooed on his belly do a little dance, smile and say "No thankya, matie" and keep movin').

More than any other type of nightlife destination, this is where you go to get yourself into a good mood, pronto. Whether you've been fighting with your man, having a hard time at work, or just have the general sense that everything is out of control, the neighborhood pub is part therapist, part chocolate cake. A half-hour of sitting, sipping, and spilling your guts to your friends or whomever else will listen while all around you people play darts, tell jokes, talk politics, and laugh at anything even remotely funny is all it takes to make it seem like, somehow, everything will be all right. Or if not, your life still couldn't be as bad as poor old Mick's, now could it? Lucky you if you're already in a great mood when you get there, because now life's just going to get better.

It's true that some pubs have a distinctly "guys-only feel," which can make a girl feel like a fish out of water—or worse, a fish being dangled over the side of the pool at the Sea World's spectacular killer-whale show. But those dives are easy to avoid. You'll usually get the mega-machismo vibe the second you walk in. In general, the more windows, lights, and chicks in the place, the better the chances you're not walking into a drug den or unofficial Hell's Angels headquarters (though, for the record, most Hell's Angels are very nice guys).

No neighborhood bar is complete without dartboards, pool tables, and TVs that have been channeling ESPN since the day they were installed. So the more you know about how to hit a bull's-eye, get a ball in the corner pocket, and talk like a fan, the more you're going to have in common with handsome strangers. In this chapter you'll find tips on all of the above, plus some key things you need to know about the heart and soul of every pub: beer!

The Cocktail: Poor Man's Black Velvet

Description This delicious sweet and bitter combo is an Irish favorite. To make a "Rich Man's Black Velvet," fill a champagne flute with equal parts bubbly and Guinness.

Ingredients
Hard cider
Guinness

Directions Fill a pint glass half full with hard cider and then gently fill to the top with Guinness by pouring the beer over the back of a spoon.

—recipe courtesy of Milano's in New York, New York

The Cocktail: Depth Charge

Description Make like a dock worker and chug this ballsy drink before it overflows the glass and gets all over your Diesel jeans (dock workers wear Diesel, right?).

Ingredients
1 shot of whiskey
⅔ pint beer

Directions Drop the shot of whiskey (shot glass and all) into a pint glass filled two-thirds with beer. Drink immediately.
—recipe courtesy of The Walnut Brewery in Boulder, Colorado

JUNGLE BASICS

Beer 101

Ladies, there's a lot of beer out there, and not just in terms of quantity. "From pale ales to dark stouts, there must be 60 different ways of brewing beer," says Julie Johnson, editor of *All About Beer* magazine. "And each method produces a beverage with a unique color, taste, and texture." There's no doubt that light lagers—Budweiser, Coors, Michelob, Miller, Amstel, Beck, Heineken, and Fosters to name a few—are the most popular, but that doesn't mean they're the best. Not by a long shot. "Though a light lager can be refreshing on a hot day, there are so many delicious beers available, you shouldn't spend too much time drinking that mostly tasteless, yellow, gassy stuff." Johnson suggests going to a beer festival (check www.beerfestivals.org to find one near you on any given month) and sampling as many types as you can find to figure out what you like best. In the meantime, here are six facts you need to know to be truly brew-savvy.

Barley is the basic ingredient in beer.

One of the first steps in brewing is to germinate barley (which means to moisten barley seeds and cause them to develop). The barley grains are allowed to sprout ever so slightly, and then heat is applied to stop the growth. The heat roasts the barley, which is now called "malt." This is the point at which the color of a beer will be determined. The longer you roast the malt, the darker the beer will be. Water, yeast, and hops are all added later.

A beer is either a lager, an ale, or a rare combination of the two.

The only difference is in the yeast that is used during fermentation and the temperature at which that fermentation takes place. Ales originated in England and Belgium. They are fermented at warmer temperatures, using yeast that adds a large variety of interesting flavors to the beer. Lagers originated in Central Europe, and are fermented at cooler temperatures using yeast that creates crisper, less complex flavors.

Dark beers aren't stronger or more fattening than light beers.

Dark beers are often more flavorful than light ones, but they don't necessarily contain more alcohol. The number of calories and amount of alcohol in a pint of Guinness are the same as in a pint of Bud.

Brown bottles are better.

If you've ever thought a beer that came in a clear or green glass bottle smelled or tasted "skunky," you were exactly right. Hops are spices that are added to beer to give it its bitterness, and to preserve it. They are very sensitive to light. If too much light hits the hops for even a small amount of time,

a chemical compound is created that's very similar to the one skunks emit. Only brown glass bottles protect a beer from becoming skunked.

Guinness is different because of the nitrogen.
Most beers flow from the keg, through the tubes, and out the tap because there's enough pressure from trapped carbon dioxide inside the keg to push it along. If there isn't, more CO_2 is added. But Guinness and some other beers like Boddington's add nitrogen to the CO_2 to push the beer from the keg to the tap. Nitrogen bubbles are much smaller and dissolve differently, creating that creamy texture and white frothy head you get with a Guinness.

When in doubt, ask for whatever is local.
Beer is best when it's fresh, and beer that comes from nearby is likely to be the freshest.

For more info about beer, check out www.allaboutbeer.com

MATING CALLS

Attract a Foxy Fan
Looking for love at a sports bar? Drop these lines while watching the game and guys are bound to be impressed.

The Sport: Hockey
The strategy: When hockey players get lazy (which happens at least two or three times in a match), they'll stop passing the puck carefully from player to player and will start smacking it as hard as they can toward the goal and then skating after it, wherever it happens to end up. When you notice this happening, get within earshot of a hot male fan and say "Man, that is dump and chase hockey!" He'll probably ask you to marry him.

The Sport: Basketball

The strategy: Wait until the point guard of the losing team has the ball (he's easy to spot because he dribbles the ball down the court after the other team has scored), and say disapprovingly "Hmmph. That guy is no Jason Kidd." Nearby babes will grunt in agreement because Kidd is the best point guard in the NBA. Just be careful not to say it while watching the New Jersey Nets.

The Sport: Football

The strategy: Stand behind the hunky viewer of your choice, then scour the screen for the hugest guy on the field (let's say it's number 72). The next time the camera focuses on him, say "Damn. Number 72 is built like a brick shit-house!" Extra points if you can say "Damn" like Martin Lawrence.

The Sport: Baseball

The strategy: Mosey up to a hottie watching the game and ask what only someone who cares about baseball would want to know: "What's the count?" He'll respond with two numbers which will be the number of balls (bad pitches, not male body parts) followed by the number of strikes. A "full count" is "3 and 2," which means there have been three balls and two strikes.

THE MANLY DRINK YOU SHOULD TRY: BUNRATTY POTCHEEN

This clear, powerful spirit has been around longer than whiskey and vodka and has as much alcohol in it as Bacardi 151°. But that's not the coolest thing about Potcheen (the names comes from the word "poitín" in Gaelic which means "little pot"). What makes it particularly badass is that it's both made and outlawed in Ireland. Since 1661, it's been condemned as moonshine and illegal to consume anywhere on the island. By an odd legal twist, it is legal to export the stuff, and it's just now making its way to the United States. Because of its high alcohol content, Potcheen is fun to drink, but watch out, because it tastes like something a bunch of excommunicated leprechauns would cook up in a rusty metal tub down by the river. Invite your Irish date back to your place and serve it over ice or try it in place of vodka in a Bloody Mary. (Look on www.avimports.com to find a store near you that sells it.)

The Cocktail: Bloody Mary

Description A favorite amongst a.m. drinkers, even the smallest pubs will keep a few cans of tomato juice on hand for the sole purpose of making this standard cocktail.

Ingredients

1 ½ oz. vodka

2 dashes of salt

3 dashes of Tabasco

3–4 oz. tomato juice

Directions Shake with ice then strain over ice in a highball glass. Garnish by squeezing a lime over the drink then dropping it in and adding a pickled green bean.

—recipe courtesy of The Columns in New Orleans, Louisiana

The Cocktail: Fuzzy Navel

Description Yummier than a screwdriver (vodka and OJ), a Fuzzy Navel is most certainly a girlie drink. But it's still simple enough that a grizzled bartender won't mind making it.

Ingredients

1 ½ oz. peach schnapps

4 oz. orange juice

Directions Pour schnapps and OJ over ice in a highball glass.

—recipe courtesy of The Owl 'n' Thistle Irish Pub in Seattle, Washington

The Cocktail: Long Island Iced Tea

Description Yes, it looks like something you'd throw together while raiding your parents' liquor cabinet, but it tastes surprisingly good. Order it for a guy when you want him to end up in the palm of your hand.

Ingredients

¼ oz. rum

¼ oz. gin

¼ oz. vodka

¼ oz. triple sec

¼ oz. tequila

¾ oz. fresh lemon juice

Chilled Coke

Directions Pour all measured ingredients over ice in a highball glass then add Coke until it becomes tea colored. Stir well. Garnish with an orange slice.

—recipe courtesy of Halligan Bar in Detroit, Michigan

FIELD GUIDE TO GUYS

Species: The Blue-Collar Babe

Common Physical Traits: Broken-in jeans, gray or blue T-shirt or Gap sweater, Swiss Army watch, finger-combed hair, a rough shave

Scent: Ivory soap and Right Guard

Animal Behavior: Shows off at pool or darts to try and get a woman's attention or chugs beer until he gets up the guts to tell her she's pretty.

Natural Habitat: The Neighborhood Pub

Tips for the Blue-Collar Babe Hunter: Tell him that you and your friends are looking for a couple of guys to cream at pool.

What You'll Get for Your Birthday: A mountain bike

JUNGLE SOUNDS

What's on the Jukebox at a Neighborhood Pub

These crowd pleasers are highly likely to turn up in corner bars from Boston to San Francisco—because they're practically part of our DNA. They're the tunes you end up singing in the shower at the top of your lungs.

"Paint It Black" by The Rolling Stones
"Welcome to the Jungle" by Guns 'n' Roses
"Don't Get Me Wrong" by The Pretenders
"Born to Run" by Bruce Springsteen
"Sex Machine" by James Brown
"Dyer Maker" by Led Zeppelin
"Like a Rolling Stone" by Bob Dylan
"Come Dancing" by The Kinks
"I Want to Be Sedated" by The Ramones
"Just a Gigolo" by David Lee Roth
"Crazy for You" by Madonna
"Little Pink Houses" by John Cougar Mellencamp
"Running Down a Dream" by Tom Petty
"Blaze of Glory" by Bon Jovi
"The Tide Is High" by Blondie
"Smells Like Teen Spirit" by Nirvana
"Sweet Jane" by The Velvet Underground
"Changes" by David Bowie
"Should I Stay or Should I Go" by The Clash
"Stay Up Late" by The Talking Heads

The Cocktail: Gin or Vodka Gimlet

Description It tastes as good as a fancy cocktail but doesn't require any of the fuss. Sharp lime juice makes it tough to taste the liquor.

Ingredients
1 ½ oz. gin or vodka
½ oz. lime juice

Directions Pour ingredients into a rocks glass filled with ice. Stir well and garnish with a wedge of lime. For a sweeter version, stir in a teaspoon of powdered sugar.

—recipe courtesy of Manuel's Tavern in Atlanta, Georgia

JUNGLE MOVES

Kick Butt at Bar Games

Maybe this should be called "Get By at Bar Games," since to kick butt at anything you'd have to practice —and no busy babe in her right mind is going to spend her spare time practicing darts and billiards. So, here's a mini-lesson on the basic moves. After that, just go with the flow.

How to Throw a Dart

1. Holding the dart in your dominant hand and stand flat-footed with your knees locked.

2. Lift your arm so that your upper arm is parallel to the floor and your forearm is parallel to the wall on which the dartboard is hanging. (Don't put your arm out to the side as if you're throwing a baseball— keep it at a right angle to your chest.)

3. Keep your upper arm steady, but shake out your wrist so that it's nice and loose. When throwing the

dart, you want your wrist to snap forward quickly, so it shouldn't be tense.

4. Keep your eyes pinned to the spot on the dartboard that you want to hit.

5. Moving only your elbow and your wrist, throw the dart toward the board. Start out by throwing the dart in an arc. As you get better you'll start to throw it faster and straighter.

Source: Glenn Remick, President of the American Darters Association (www.adadarters.com)

How to Hit a Pool Ball

1. Find your shot. Look for a ball with an open path to both the white cue ball and a pocket (you can start bouncing the cue ball off of walls and other fancy stuff later on). Now mentally draw a straight line from the center of that ball to the center of the pocket into which you want the ball to go. Pretend the line extends straight through the ball. The point where the line comes out on the other side is exactly where you want the cue ball to hit; let's call that point X.

2. Position yourself so that you'll be able to hit X with the cue ball by propelling the cue ball in a perfectly straight line.

3. Stand with your feet shoulder length apart and with one foot slightly further back for balance. Keep your legs straight and, when you bend, bend at the waist.

4. Hold the cue stick with your dominant hand and put your other hand palm down on the pool table about five to ten inches away from the cue ball.

5. Raise your palm an inch or two off of the table, keeping your fingers stiff, and lift your thumb to create a crease between your thumb and the side of your hand. Lay the business end of the cue in the crease (which is called the "bridge"). Try sliding the stick back and forth in the crease. It should slide smoothly and evenly.

6. Steady yourself, pull the cue stick back, and hit the cue ball at its center. If you aimed correctly, it should hit X and send the numbered ball rolling toward and into the pocket.

Source: www.poolplayers.com

The Cocktail: Whiskey Sour

Description When you order this tart drink in a pub, you'll get a blend of whiskey and sour mix, but use sugar and fresh-squeezed lemon juice to make a more upscale version at home.

Ingredients
2 oz. blended whiskey
Juice of ½ of a lemon
½ tsp. powdered sugar

Directions Shake all ingredients with ice and strain into a rocks glass over ice. Garnish with a cherry.
—recipe courtesy of The Village Idiot in New York, New York

JUNGLE LOOKS

What to Wear to a Neighborhood Bar

The Joan Jett: Pull on a tight black T-shirt (if only you could find one that says "bad girl" in small white letters) and a pair of jeans. Add rock accessories like a studded belt and lots of heavy silver and black leather jewelry.

The College Cutie: It's the outfit frat boys love: jeans or cords and a tank top. Yes, it's simple—that's why the simple-minded like it.

The J. Lo: Got a pair of extra low-rise, stretch jeans and a crop top? If you want to cause a commotion amongst the male patrons without looking overdressed, that's the way to go. Just bring a sweatshirt to put on in case you get tired of getting all of your drinks for free.

The Pretty Prep: A jean skirt and a button-down oxford shirt may sound prim, but there's something charming and understated about it that always goes over well.

The Yoga Vixen: Unlike most other bars, going to a pub after (or instead) of the gym is perfectly acceptable. You'll look laid-back and buff in a pair of yoga pants and a zip-up hoodie.

JUNGLE TALES

Making Old Friends

"My work friends and I would always go to this one English pub on Wednesday nights, and every time we were there we saw the same crazy old British lady who would push her dentures out with her tongue and then suck them back in. One night she came out of the ladies' room screaming and crying about how she'd lost her teeth. I don't know why she picked me, but she grabbed my arm and asked me to help her find them. She was hysterical, so I went into the ladies' room and they were just lying there in the sink. I used a few paper towels to pick them up and brought them out to her. She was so happy, she hugged me and told everyone what a sweet girl I was. Then this Hugh Grant look-alike came out of nowhere and started thanking me profusely and offering to buy me a beer. He was the owner of the bar and the crazy lady was his grandmother." —Winona, 34

JUNGLE PARTY

How to Host a Beer Tasting

Drink Menu

To make a beer tasting interesting, you're going to need at least five different styles of beer (to make things even more interesting, consider getting two different brands of each style). That means a trip to one of those beer mega-stores to find a large selection of microbrews. Before going, log onto www.spiritjournal.com/beerguide, where you'll find descriptions of 28 different styles of beer. Get a few bottles of each kind that you choose for tasting, and then stock up on a less expensive light lager for people to drink when the tasting is over. Some styles to try: Amber, Brown Ale, India Pale Ale, Pilsner, Porter, Steam Beer, Stout, Wheat.

Glassware and Garnish

Diehard beer lovers will argue against using plastic cups, but unless you want to spend the whole night washing glasses there really isn't a good alternative. Buy the smallest, sturdiest cups you can find for tasting, and then some larger ones for whatever light lager you'll be serving afterwards. You don't need garnish, but you will need plenty of water and munchies to clear people's palates between gulps. Bread, crackers, or popcorn work best.

Decorations

Forget about decorating and consider Scotch-guarding your furniture. With that many cups of beer going around, there are bound to be endless spills. If you want to get creative, you could transform one room of your pad into a German beer garden. Buy fake ivy and tape it to the walls so that it looks like the outside of an old building. Cut large pieces of cardboard into tree trunks and add big construction paper blobs of green as leaves. If you have a beach umbrella, prop it up over your kitchen table. Tape a sign to your door that says "Willkommen!" and grill up some bratwurst to feed your guests.

Another idea is to go with a college-drinking theme and tell everyone to wear a T-shirt or sweatshirt with the name of their alma mater on it. You could cover the walls of your apartment with the posters that everyone had hanging up in their dorm rooms (Bob Marley, Jim Morrison, The Grateful Dead, John Lennon, assorted supermodels, Ansel Adams and Herb Ritts prints, etc.), and serve Ramen noodles and Pop Tarts as party food. Yeah, it's a little pathetic, but it's a reason to drink, isn't it?

Lighting

If you're going with the beer garden theme, you're supposed to be outdoors basking in the European sunshine, so there's no need to dim the lights.

Considering that most dorm rooms have horrible fluorescent lighting, you don't need to light candles for the college look either—although you could pick up a lava lamp for atmosphere.

Audio and Visuals

A great background movie option for the German beer garden party is National Lampoon's *European Vacation* (1985), which features a bunch of scenes at an Oktoberfest celebration. Or opt for a hokey Germany travel video from some bygone decade. Add sound with a compilation of Oktoberfest tunes like *Oktoberfest in Germany* (Delta, 1999), or a polka album like *Polkas & Waltzes* by The Happy Glad Polka Band (Bellaire Records, 1999).

For collegiate entertainment, play the two quintessential fraternity flicks: *Revenge of the Nerds* (1984) and *Animal House* (1978), and mercilessly blast the albums that were most popular between your freshman and senior years.

WHAT YOUR DRINK SAYS ABOUT YOUR PERSONALITY

Like sneakers, handbags, and hairstyles, what you order at the bar has a way of revealing a little something about your personality and/or current mood. Here's what flashes through other people's minds when you ask for a . . .

Beer
The Levi's® of beverages, a girl who orders a beer is out for a no-fuss, no-rush night (unless you're chugging it, that is). The cheaper or more local the beer, the more chill and down-to-earth you seem. People will see you as more relaxed and approachable than chicks holding something pink and fancy.

Girlie Martini
From Cosmopolitans to Sour-Apple Martinis, these fashionable libations hold loads of liquor but are still very feminine. Onlookers will peg you as a fun party girl who likes to pamper herself. Guys will be equal parts intimidated and fascinated (they'll assume that you smell very, very good).

Vodka Martini
The signature drink of the successful—and slightly stressed—executive, a vodka martini is all business, baby. With one of these in your hand you'll seem confident, powerful, and sexy—and like you want a nice buzz, now!

Vodka or Gin and Tonic
Ordering such a straightforward and classic drink makes you come across as a straightforward, classic gal. You probably prefer simple pleasures and are perfectly comfortable being you—an extremely attractive quality.

Margarita
If tequila is your drink tonight, you must be out to let off some steam—especially if you ordered a pitcher. Guys at the bar will expect you and your group of

friends to be having the most fun of anyone there. Don't be surprised if they try desperately to get your attention.

Glass of Wine

With wine in your glass, you look like a Meg Ryan romantic. Everyone from the bartender to the guy next to you will figure you're out for a nice quiet night and some good conversation. You'll attract more older men than diehard party boys.

Umbrella Drink

You've gotta be celebrating something. And if your drink is silly, that means you're in the mood to be, too. People can't help but smile at you when they see you sipping on something big, frozen, and blue, and flirty guys are bound to ask what the happy occasion is.

Whiskey on the Rocks

Of all possible drinks, this one is the most Rock 'n' Roll for a woman to ask for. You'll give off a tough, been-there-done-that vibe that can only be described as very cool. A brave guy might ask you to play pool, light his cigarette, or arm-wrestle.

The Latest Lounge

Pssst... see that girl over there on the zebra-print couch by the reflecting pool? She's dating the lead singer of that new teeny-bopper boyband. He isn't even old enough to drink so she has to party without him. The guy standing next to her under the skylight? A real live prince--or at least he used to be. His monarchy was just overthrown and he was forced to seek political asylum in LA. And that skinny guy with the long curly hair who just ordered another bottle of champagne? Son of a bigtime designer. I just saw his photo in the Style section. Hey, isn't that the model who was just on the cover of Vogue walking toward the bathroom?

If you've been to one of the "in" places in a big city, you know that celeb-spottings are common and gossip reigns supreme. Once you're there, you can spend the whole night doing nothing but pointing and whispering and end up having a blast. But there's a lot more to luxe partying than stealing glances at A-listers. From the fabric of the designer chairs to the curve of the bar to the totally unique cocktail in your glass, every detail of an upscale lounge is crafted to exude pleasure. Designers have slaved over the colors, textures, and shapes to build a space that feels edgy, extravagant, and incredibly hip. A mixologist has painstakingly put together a list of libations that will impress even the fussiest cocktail fan. Which is why the Latest Lounge is where we go when we want to be pampered. It's the place to be because simply being there surrounded by the flashy sights, sounds, and chatter is stimulation enough. The environment is so intoxicating, you probably won't need more than one cocktail to start feeling tipsy—a good thing since they're probably $12 or $16 a pop.

If there's a model for a trendy bar, it's Lot 61 in New York, which has somehow retained its elite status in spite of the fact that it's been around for years. The lounge is located in a warehouse district (packed with cheap real estate, the artists migrate there first, followed by the scenesters), and with 5,000 square feet of breathing room, it has plenty of atmosphere. Works by internationally acclaimed artists hang on the walls, sculpted rubber chairs that were found in a 1940s insane asylum are clustered around tables, and sliding partitions create instant walls for private parties or make the space more intimate on slow nights. There's also a fireplace, a DJ booth, and a menu of 61 martinis to choose from. On any given night, you're likely to see faces you recognize from movies and magazines. But Lot 61 isn't so exclusive that you can't get in—a great dress and a little velvet-rope know-how, and you'll have no trouble at all. Other bars go to ridiculous extremes to keep out everyone but the upper crust of fashionistas and power-people. They'll have no sign, no phone number, and a no-entry policy—unless you have a password or electronic keycard given to you by the owner. And the second the word gets out, the place is considered ruined. Of course, to some, that makes it even more thrilling if you happen to end up inside.

Exorbitant cover charges are another bane of the swanky bar, but it's easy to argue that the cost is worth it—once in a while. There are simply far too few places on this earth that feel this fabulous, and life is far too short to not visit them. Besides, where else are you going to show off those Jimmy Choo heels that you bought on a whim? Live it up, baby!

The Cocktail: Granny Apple Martini

Description It started as a fad, but the Apple Martini is so good no one wants to let it go. With more apple juice than liquor, this is a lighter version than most.

Ingredients

2 oz. sour apple liqueur
1 oz. citrus-infused vodka

Tiny splash of sour mix
4 oz. apple juice

Directions Shake with ice and strain into a chilled martini glass. Garnish with a slice of apple and a maraschino cherry.

—recipe courtesy of Modern in Washington, DC

The Cocktail: The White Cosmo

Description The clear version of the Cosmo is fun to order because it still tastes sweet and girlie, but it looks like a straitlaced gin martini.

Ingredients

2 oz. citrus-infused vodka

5 oz. white cranberry juice

½ oz. fresh lime juice

½ tsp. powdered sugar

Lime twist

Directions Shake all ingredients except lime twist with ice and strain into a martini glass. Garnish with a lime twist.

—recipe courtesy of Sugar Bar in New York, New York

JUNGLE BASICS

Bubbly 101

It's the choice drink of rock stars and socialites alike and the most glamorous beverage of all time. Whether you're ordering a champagne-based cocktail or a bottle for the table, here's what you should know.

Champagne vs. Sparkling

Bubbly that's called "champagne" can only come from the Champagne region of France. Though some sparkling wines from California are made in the same traditional way as champagne, they're still considered sparkling wines. The French call sparkling wine made in any other part of France Vins Mousseux. Italian bubbly is called Asti Spumante. The Spanish version is Cava, and the Germans call their sparking wine Sekt.

The Methode Champenoise

These words on the label mean that the sparkling wine or champagne has been made according to traditional methods which involve a second fermentation process that happens inside the bottle. This method produces smaller bubbles and a more delicate taste. Anything else is just carbonated wine.

Sweet vs. Dry

The following terms are used to describe how sweet a sparkling wine is or isn't. To tell the difference between one level and the next you'd have to try very hard, but jump from one end of the list to the other and the change becomes obvious. "Extra-Dry" isn't the most dry because when the French created it, they couldn't imagine that anyone would request champagne that was any less sweet than that. But they did. So they made it and called it Brut. Then it happened again, and they called it Brut Nature.

Doux: Extremely sweet
Demi-Sec, Dry: Very sweet
Sec: Noticeably sweet
Extra Dry: Just a hint of sweetness
Brut: Not sweet at all
Brut Nature: Bone dry

Just Your Size

The little individual-sized bottles of champagne (187ml) that are showing up everywhere are called splits. Drink your split with a straw to avoid messing up your lipstick.

Vintage vs. Non-vintage (NV)

Champagne vineyards sometimes decide to call particularly good champagne harvests a "vintage" year. You'll know it's a vintage if there's a year on the label. Otherwise it's a "non-vintage," which means a blend of different harvests. Vintages are special, but great champagne doesn't have to be one. (The highest-quality and most expensive champagne available from any brand is called a Vintage "Prestige." It's made from the first pressing of the best grapes and aged longer than usual.)

White vs. Pink

Most champagne is white, but Rosé Champagne attains a soft pink color from the skin of the pinot grapes it's made from. Roses are usually made in the Brut (dry) style, and even though "pink champagne" has a cheesy rep, connoisseurs consider it to be perfectly respectable bubbly.

Flute vs. Wineglass

Champagne is usually served in a tulip-shaped glass because the small surface area on the bottom of the glass causes the bubbles to escape more slowly—and because a champagne flute has become a symbol of a celebration. But frequent champagne drinkers use a wineglass instead and, if you like champagne, there's no reason not to drink it like you would any other white wine.

Don't Launch the Cork

There's no need to put someone's eye out and lose precious bubbles. Loosen the cork slowly with one hand while you point the bottle away from you and brace it against your body. The cork should give with a whisper, not a pop.

Source: Gary Heck, owner and president of Korbel (www.korbel.com)

The Cocktail: Blueberry Mojito

Description Mint is what makes a mojito so good, but blueberries make it even better. It's so fresh and summery, it's like a cotton sundress in a glass.

Ingredients

8 mint leaves

8 blueberries

2 oz. lemon-flavored rum

½ oz. simple syrup

3 oz. club soda

Juice of 1 lime wedge

Directions Muddle mint and blueberries with a splash of soda in cocktail shaker. Add ice, rum, lime juice, and simple syrup. Shake and strain over ice in a rocks glass. Add soda. Garnish with a mint leaf and two blueberries.

—recipe courtesy of Blue Fin in New York, New York

MATING CALLS

Five Ways to Lure a (Ditzy) Male Model

Lure #1: Stand with your back to him and shout to a friend "I can't believe what a hard time my friend the casting agent is having finding a young male actor to star opposite Harvey Keitel."

Lure #2: Pop out one of the iron pills from your birth control pack and slip it into his palm while winking and smiling. Tell him that if he doesn't feel fantastic in five minutes, he should come over and start kissing you—that's what'll really make it kick in.

Lure #3: Walk up to him as if trying to remember his face and ask "Weren't you in my infectious diseases seminar in medical school?" He'll be thrilled that you mistook him for someone intelligent and gainfully employed.

Lure #4: Scooch up next to him and start to slap your hand against his butt as if you're wiping something off of his designer pants. Say "I'm so sorry, there was just this awful thing on your fantastic pants and I felt compelled to get it off for you. I didn't mean to spank you. Although now that I have, tell me, how did it feel?"

Lure #5: Offer him free liquor. Show him the two Pomegranate Martinis you're holding and say "I just bought myself and my friend one of these, and it turns out she hates pomegranates, in spite of the fact that they're delicious. Do you or one of your equally gorgeous male friends want it?"

THE MANLY DRINK TO TRY: TEQUILA AND SQUIRT

Instead of ordering a Jack and Coke, guys in Mexico City order a Tequila and Squirt. As it happens, the latter tastes a hell of a lot better, which is why the easy, breezy beverage is catching on in New York and Los Angeles.

To make it, salt the rim of a rocks glass, fill it with ice, and pour in 1 ½ oz. blue agave blanco tequila and 5 oz. Squirt (a.k.a. grapefruit soda). Add a squeeze of lime, and down it like one of the boys.

The Cocktail: Fiamma

Description A very palatable martini that smells like a berry patch and hits you like a brick.

Ingredients
1 ½ oz. Stoli Razberi
¾ oz. Cointreau
1 oz. white cranberry juice

Directions Shake with ice and strain into a martini glass. Garnish with a raspberry.

—recipe courtesy of Fiamma in New York, New York

FIELD GUIDE TO GUYS

Species: The Hipster

Common Physical Traits: $300 jeans, $12 vintage shirt, old-school sneakers or black leather ankle boots, thick-rimmed glasses, retro haircut, too-small designer sweater or hooded sweatshirt

Scent: Marc Jacobs Perfume for Men

Animal Behavior: Discussing local bands, DJs, or his latest freelance gig; lounging across couches looking bored, silently hoping women will come talk to him

Natural Habitat: The Latest Lounge

Tips for the Hipster Hunter: Melt his ultra-cool façade with a warm, friendly smile, and ask if he's ever tried your favorite trendy cocktail—whatever it happens to be.

What You'll Get for Your Birthday: Concert tickets

JUNGLE SOUNDS

Most trendy music comes and goes but these albums have long-lasting cred with the Latest Lounge crowd.

Daft Punk *Homework* (EMD/Virgin, 1997)
This breakthrough record is a combo of gritty funk, trance-inducing house, and a touch of techno. It was one of the first records to bring the complex electronic blends that were being created on club turntables to the mainstream. You'll definitely recognize two or three tracks.

Massive Attack *Mezzanine* (EMD/Virgin, 1998)
Influenced by Motown, soul, and hip-hop, Massive Attack gave birth to what is now known as trip-hop—not that anyone could define exactly what that is. Don't let the aggressive name dissuade you, Massive Attack is a lot sexier than it is aggressive.

Orbital *Orbital 2* (London/Sire, 1992)
If you haven't heard a lot of electronica, this is the CD to try. It's a smorgasbord of electronic music—some tracks are warm and emotional with uplifting anthems, others sound cold, precise, and robotic. Somewhere in there, you'll find something to love.

Mr. Scruff *Keep It Unreal* (Ninja Tune, 1999)
The kids went wild for this DJ's mind-blowing mix of every genre of music known to man. Andrew Carthy (a.k.a. Mr. Scruff) ties it all together with a heavy bass sound that keeps your body moving. Great for partygoers with low attention spans.

Thievery Corporation *Sounds From the Verve Hi-Fi* (ESL/1997)
Usually categorized under "trance" or "ambient," Eric Hilton and Rob Garza, the two guys behind Thievery Corporation, are more like alchemists than

musicians. They experiment freely with every sound they can get their hands on to make spacey lounge music that's fun to get lost in.

Goldie *Incredible Sound of Drum 'n' Bass* (Sony/Columbia, 1999)
Flashing his crooked 24-karat smile everywhere he went, Goldie gave drum 'n' bass/jungle a face (a very scary face) when he hit the scene with *Timeless* in 1995. On this compilation, he picked the top tracks he could find, which turn out to be powerful, dark, and relentlessly thumping.

THE DJ MINI-DICTIONARY

If you want to mingle with the hot young thugs crowded around the DJ booth, you're going to have to sling some lingo.

Backspin: When a DJ spins a record backwards or alternately plays the same part of the same record on two turntables.

Beat Matching: Playing two different records at the same time so that their beats are perfectly synchronized.

Break: A brief pause in the music that comes before a change to the main beat that can be either subtle or dramatic.

Breakbeat: When a DJ interrupts standard techno four-four beats to create more unexpected, interesting rhythms.

Build: The part of the song that builds tension and energy, usually through repetition and increased volume and/or speed.

Decks: Turntables.

Downbeat: The first beat of a "loop." So if a four-beat loop is 1-2-3-4-1-2-3-4-1 . . . the downbeat will be on one. Loops typically consist of 16 beats.

Layering: Overlapping songs and/or sounds.

Loop: A piece of sound that's repeated over and over again in a sequence.

Sample: A sound or snippet of music taken from anywhere.

Scratching: The act of moving the needle back and forth along a groove in a record.

Train Wreck: When a DJ screws up and plays two tracks that don't synch with each other.

Turntablist: Someone who uses turntables and records as instruments to create new sounds.

The Cocktail: White Chocolate Raspberry

Description This is the cocktail equivalent of biting into a gourmet chocolate-covered cherry.

Ingredients

1 ¼ oz. raspberry vodka

½ oz. white chocolate liqueur

¼ oz. white creme de cacao

Splash of heavy cream

Directions Moisten the edge of a martini glass by dragging an orange slice around the rim then dip it in cinnamon sugar. Shake ingredients with ice and strain into the martini glass.

—recipe courtesy of Thin in San Diego, California

The Cocktail: Kir Royale Kiss

Description A bit of brandy makes this classic cocktail extra smooth. Its full, rich flavor is for tongues that appreciate the finer things.

Ingredients

5 oz. sparkling wine or champagne

1 oz. brandy

2 splashes of black raspberry liqueur

Directions Pour champagne into a large martini glass. Slowly stir in brandy and raspberry liqueur.

—recipe courtesy of Korbel

JUNGLE MOVES

Beat the Velvet Ropes

Play the Name Game

There are a few different strategies for getting your name on the sacred door scroll. 1) Some lounges have phone numbers you can call if you want to be listed as a guest. Call and ask. 2) Call the lounge or club and say that you're planning on coming by with four or five friends and would like to reserve a table and be put on the guest list. Assure her that you're going to be dropping some cash by asking if they serve champagne by the bottle. 3) Use your company's name. Call as a busy executive and explain that you have some important clients coming into town and would love to take them to that lounge (better yet, call and pretend to be your own assistant). 3) Do a web search with the lounge's name to find out if there's someplace online where you can put yourself on the list. Several party-promoters also have sites that provide access to guest lists. 4) After waiting in line one night, ask the bouncer how you might get your name on the list next time. He might just tell you.

Put Time on Your Side

Clubs want to fill up as fast as possible but the bulk of the lounge crowd doesn't go out until after 10 p.m., so the earlier you go the more desperate they'll be to get warm bodies inside. They might nonetheless make you wait for a few minutes just to put on a show (and give the impression that the place is already packed), but you'll get in fairly quickly.

Use Your Girl Power

It's a well-known fact that women get into bars faster when there aren't any guys with them. According to bouncers, it's a bit of a catch-22: they want a lot of male customers (who drink more and therefore spend more money) but men won't stay long at a lounge that isn't full of women, so they let as many women in as possible first and then start admitting groups of guys. Once the club is 50/50 they start letting in only women again.

Flaunt Your Style

Lounges want to maintain their reputation for attracting highly fashionable people, which means they're eager to get highly fashionable people inside. That's why wearing a head-turning outfit is guaranteed to get you ushered through the door. "Head-turning" could mean funky and original, expensive and chic, or just plain slutty. Your choice.

Be the Bouncer's Buddy

When you first arrive, walk right up to the bouncer, flash him a big smile, say hello, and ask (in a curious, not pushy way) what things are like in the club tonight. If he starts chatting, try to keep the conversation going for as long as you can. You want him to get a good look at your face so that when he sees you again he'll recognize you. And if he happens to like your smile, he just might let you and your friends through on the spot.

Stay In-the-Know

Keep your cocktail conversation ahead of the curve by clicking on these sites a few times a week.

www.dailycandy.com

Reporting from New York, Los Angeles, and London, Daily Candy posts alerts about the latest trends in food and drink, fashion, beauty, fun, arts and culture around town. The only problem is trying not to blow your entire paycheck on glam goodies only a starlet would need—like a miniature dog collar that doubles as a cell phone and a personal massager.

www.trendcentral.com

Like Daily Candy, Trend Central offers insider tips on everything new, but it's more about what the hipster kids are up to now than which hairdresser in Soho gives the best bob. You'll find Hollywood gossip hiding on the pages, and there are city guides to 15 top towns with updates on which neighborhoods are hot and what's currently in the air.

The Cocktail: Strawberry Lemon Drop

Description A hint of amaretto and cranberry make this libation deliciously different.

Ingredients

1 ¼ oz. strawberry-flavored vodka
¾ oz. amaretto
2 oz. sweet and sour mix

Splash of cranberry juice
Juice of 3 lemon wedges
1 sugar packet

Directions Shake with ice and strain into a sugar-rimmed martini glass.

—recipe courtesy of Thin in San Diego, California

JUNGLE LOOKS

What to Wear to the Latest Lounge

Getting all decked out doesn't just make you the center of attention, it can get you better service. To earn the adoration of everyone from the bouncer to the bathroom attendant, take this advice from Nancy Brensson, Senior Fashion Editor at *Cosmopolitan* magazine.

"You want to stand out, and that means you're going to have to do something dramatic." Whether it's an enormous flower in your hair, a colorful scarf around your neck, or really big ethnic-looking jewelry, choose an accessory that's an eyeball magnet and you're off to a good start.

"Be original and innovative—show that you took some time putting your look together." You're not going to win any points with a J. Crew outfit in this crowd. You've got to get funky. Consider layering pieces on top of each other to create a new look. Tie a fringed shawl around your hips if you're wearing a pair of jeans or boring black pants. Wear a delicate silk camisole under a tuxedo jacket. Pick two slinky slip-dresses in solid colors and wear them one on top of the other.

"When in doubt, wear something that sparkles." Sequins are always sensational after dark. Try a sequined miniskirt with a little black top, or an itsy-bitsy shiny tank top with a pair of black satin pants.

"Catch on to the latest craze." People are going to notice if you're wearing the trendy new thing, so buy just one attention-getting new top in the latest style and wear it when you go out. So if Asian-inspired looks are in, snag an embroidered silk kimono shirt in a bright jewel tone like ruby, turquoise, or emerald. Better to spend $100 on a shirt that's absolutely stunning than $50 on a jade bracelet that no one can even see. Think big.

"You have to own at least one pair of killer heels." High, strappy heels and sexy boots carry more currency in the fashion world than any other item. Leave your Easy Spirits at home, and break out a pair of shoes that will make people gasp. And as Carrie from *Sex and the City* knows, that doesn't mean they have to be pretty. Shocking shoes can be just about anything—as long as they're at least three inches tall and unlike anything you've ever seen at the mall.

JUNGLE TALES

Dancing Fool

"I was wandering around this monstrous club in Amsterdam trying to find my friends when I ended up in a VIP room on the second floor that was entirely white. The walls, ceiling, floor, furniture, ashtrays, lights—everything was white. After circling the room, I realized my friends weren't in there so I headed toward the door. But since all the doors were white I had no idea which one I came in through. I decided to pick one at random and just walked through it.

Someone immediately grabbed my arm and started dancing with me. Upon closer inspection I realized that that someone was a guy who was wearing nothing but a leather thong and his entire body was painted with tiger stripes. I had walked onto a glass-bottomed balcony where professional dancers perform twenty feet above the crowd. The dancers grinded against me and twirled me around until I was dizzy and then nudged me back through the door into the white room. Then the bartender started yelling at me. I was getting orange and black body paint all over the white leather." —Gwynn, 25

The Cocktail: Nutty Frenchman
Description More of a dessert than a drink, this thick, luscious concoction will slide down your throat and light a fire in your belly.

Ingredients
1 ½ oz. Armagnac
½ oz. Frangelica
½ oz. clear creme de cacao

Directions Pour ingredients into a martini glass (or a brandy snifter if you have one).
—recipe courtesy of Blue Grotto in New York, New York

JUNGLE PARTY

How to Throw a Swanky Cocktail Party

Drink Menu
The White Cosmo, Blueberry Mojito, Fiamma, and Tequila and Squirt are four fab cocktails to offer together. The Cosmo is a familiar favorite for those who don't feel like venturing into unknown territory. The blueberry twist on the

Mojito will have everyone wanting to try it—even if they're sick to death of regular mojitos. The Fiamma is brand spanking new (use white cranberry juice to make it so you don't have to buy two kinds), and the Tequila and Squirt is so basic that the non-fussy drinkers in the group will love it.

Glassware and Garnish

Like all of the slickest drinks these days, two of the above recipes call for martini glasses. The other two require rocks glasses. Regardless of what glass you use, give your concoctions some cutting-edge detail by doing what a few of the trendiest bartenders have been known to do—write your first initial on the top of every cocktail you pour. Fill a squeeze bottle with a slim nozzle with black raspberry honey and Chambord and write the first letter of your name as if you were frosting a cake. If you're not an egomaniac, write the initial of the person you're making the drink for. Can't find black raspberry honey anywhere? Buy it online at www.virginiabrand.com.

Decorations

Minimalist is modern, so clean and declutter every corner of your pad. Leave large surfaces entirely bare, take down the magnets off of the fridge, stack magazines and books out of sight, and throw everything on the bathroom counter in a drawer and just leave a single bar of soap and a candle. If your walls are packed with random photographs and art, consider taking most of them down and stashing them in the closet for the night. Elegant, simple flowers like white orchids or tulips in clear glass vases will help make the place seem fresh and spare. White towels will, too. An inexpensive way to up your apartment's "designer" factor is to pick up a few funky gadgets and serving dishes (like those made by Alessi) for your kitchen and bathroom. A great place to find Alessi is www.retromodern.com.

Lighting

Tea lights always look simple and sophisticated. Line several of them up on windowsills and place them on tables by arranging them in a three by three square grid with about half an inch between each candle.

Audio and Visuals

For the absolute latest in electronic music, go straight to the source—the record labels. Check out websites like www.giantstep.com, www.metalheadz.co.uk, and www.cvibes.com to see what's up next from the independents.

The possibilities are endless for hip movies, but what could be more stylish than a little Madonna? Add some ironic visual entertainment by playing *Swept Away* (2002), her disastrous beached-babe flick, in the background. She and Adriano Giannini (unlike the guys on *The Sopranos,* this Italian is H-O-T) can roll around in the sand and smack each other all night long while you and your guests have some civilized fun. Make it a theme by playing *Body of Evidence* (1993) and *Shanghai Surprise* (1986), two more Material Girl clunkers.

DIVA-INSPIRED DRINKS

Some women are so mesmerizing, bartenders are compelled to create a libation in their honor. These unofficial cocktails will put fame and fortune on the tip of your tongue.

Madonna
(born Madonna Louise Veronica Ciccone in Bay City, Michigan)
It's easy to imagine Mrs. Ritchie sipping this drink while loitering in bobby sox and pumps outside of a pool hall back in her "Borderline" days.

Ingredients
2 oz. cherry-flavored vodka
6 oz. 7-Up
1 maraschino cherry

Directions Pour vodka and 7-Up over ice in a tall glass. Garnish with a cherry.

Mary Pickford
(born Gladys Louise Smith in Toronto, Ontario, Canada)
Mary Pickford wasn't just an actress who starred in 236 films; she also helped found United Artists Studio and the Academy of Motion Picture Arts and Sciences. The Bloody Mary was created with her in mind, as well as this rum-and-pineapple treat.

Ingredients
1 oz. light rum
1 oz. pineapple juice
¼ tsp. grenadine
¼ tsp. cherry liqueur

Directions Shake with ice and strain into a martini glass.

Scarlett O'Hara

(played by Vivien Leigh—born Vivian Mary Hartley in Darjeeling, India—in *Gone With the Wind***)**

The bratty but lovable southern belle's signature drink is ladylike but powerful. Perfect for when you want to get up the guts to slap someone silly.

Ingredients

2 oz. Southern Comfort

6 oz. cranberry juice

1 lime wedge

Directions Pour Southern Comfort over ice in a tall glass. Fill with cranberry juice. Squeeze juice of one lime on top. Stir well.

Mae West

(born in Brooklyn, New York)

Here's a cocktail named for the wittiest actress of all time. Why try it? Because brandy and sugar tastes warm and sweet, and "when choosing between two evils, I always like to pick the one I never tried before," says Mae.

Ingredients

4 oz. brandy

1 tsp. powdered sugar

Directions Shake brandy and sugar with ice then strain into a martini glass.

Bettie Page

(born in Nashville, Tennessee)

There are nights when we bad-mouth the sex kitten at the party, and then there are nights when we *are* the sex kitten at the party. This cherry-flavored cocktail, named after the queen of pinups, is for the latter.

Ingredients

1 oz. gin

1 oz. sweet vermouth

1 tsp. cherry liqueur

1 maraschino cherry

Directions Stir gin, vermouth, and cherry liqueur with ice then strain into a martini glass and garnish with a cherry.

Coco Chanel

(born Gabrielle Chanel in Saumur, France)

The inventor of the "little black dress" will always have a place in every woman's heart, so why not put her in your glass as well? Coco would have appreciated the stylish simplicity of this creamy cocktail.

Ingredients

1 oz. gin

1 oz. Kahlua

2 oz. cream

Directions Shake well with ice then strain into a martini glass.

Sources: www.about.com, www.webtender.com

The Margarita Bar

Strings of fire-engine red, jalapeño-shaped lights dangle from the ceiling, Latin tunes fill the lime-scented air, and you have to reach between someone's dancing feet to get your drink off of the bar. Welcome to margarita central. Walking into a great margarita bar should feel a little like traveling back in time to Spring Break freshman year when, if all went well, you'd party all night and wake up the next morning with tequila on your breath and a football player in your arms. To get straight to the point, this is where you should go when you want to act your age—minus ten.

In the land of Corona and Cuervo, having fun and causing trouble are intrinsically linked. That's why doing tequila shots in between drinks, chain-eating cheese-smothered nachos, and daring your best friend to throw a deep-fried jalapeño at the hottest guy in the room all seem like such great ideas when you're there. And that's exactly why we love going. No matter how professional and sophisticated we can be, there's always an immature party animal hibernating inside of us (she looks a lot like you, but she dresses like Christina Aguilera). And it feels fantastic to set her loose in a place where she'll be warmly welcomed, not to mention frequently hit on.

You might imagine that the American margarita bar was modeled after a traditional Mexican watering-hole (that *piñata is* authentic looking, isn't it?), but nothing could be further from the truth. The only thing our version has in common with an old-fashioned cantina is that they're both shrines to hardcore drinking. Otherwise, our Mexican-themed lounges are more akin to a three-village Cinco de Mayo festival than any bar you'll find south of the border. With the exception of big cities and heavy tourist areas (think Cancun), the typical drinking establishment in Frida Kahlo's homeland is a doorless cinderblock building with a dusty Cerveza Sol sign facing the road.

And Mexican women aren't even allowed in those places (which is totally unfair, but considering how sketchy such dives can get, *las señoritas* aren't exactly clamoring to get inside).

When deciding which bar you should grace with your presence, there's one quick way to separate the sublime from the sloppy. Ask the bartender if they use fresh lime juice in their drinks. Sweet and sour mix is a great shortcut for making an impromptu margarita or two at home, but when you're out for a treat you shouldn't settle for anything less than fresh-squeezed.

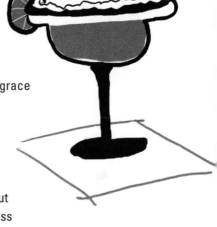

The Cocktail: Prickly Pear Margarita

Description Genuine prickly pear cactus juice makes this margarita more Mexican than most. The juice of the prickly pear is flavorful and sweet, so this cocktail is extra easy on the tongue.

Ingredients

2 ½ oz. tequila
1 ¼ oz. Grand Marnier
Juice of 1 lime

Juice of 1 lemon
1 oz. prickly pear cactus juice

Directions Shake ingredients with ice and strain into a rocks glass over ice.

—recipe courtesy of Nova in Atlanta, Georgia

The Cocktail: Raspberry Mist Margarita

Description Deceptively strong, this tangy margarita is like a WWF wrestler in a delicate pink evening gown.

Ingredients

2 oz. tequila	3 lime wedges
1 oz. raspberry liqueur (like Chambord)	Dash of powdered sugar

Directions Rim a glass with powdered sugar. Pour the tequila and raspberry liqueur in a shaker over ice. Add the juice from three lime wedges and the dash of powdered sugar. Shake well and strain into a martini glass.

—recipe courtesy of Las Margaritas Restaurant in Denver, Colorado

JUNGLE BASICS

Tequila 101

Tequila is made by distilling the juices of the "blue agave," a succulent desert-growing plant that looks a lot like a giant Aloe Vera. By law, tequila can only be made in a few Mexican villages, most of which are located in the western state of Jalisco. Before 1998, when a huge storm wiped out more than half of Jalisco's crops, all tequila had to be 100% agave. But after the storm, the Mexican government allowed distillers to produce misto (Spanish for "mixed") tequila that is composed of 60% agave and 40% Sousa, a harsh-tasting alcohol made from sugar cane. As a result, most inexpensive tequilas are misto. But the really good stuff is still 100% agave. The process of making tequila consists of cutting out the heart of the agave plant, steaming it to soften the plant fibers and extract the sugars and starches which are then fermented in a tank until all of the CO_2 has evaporated. Then yeast, which turns the sugars into alcohol, is added, after which the tequila is aged as long as desired.

Tequila's image has always been rough and tough—it's the one type of alcohol most likely to land you in jail.

In the 100% agave category, there are three types of tequila, and most brands offer one of each:

1. Blanco: Not aged for more than sixty days, blanco has a lot of fresh agave taste. If you really like that distinctly tequila kick, this will probably be your favorite. There are two types of blanco: white (a.k.a. silver) or gold. The only difference is in their color—they taste exactly the same.

2. Reposado: Aged anywhere from four to nine months in oak barrels, reposado has more of a mellow, woody flavor.

3. Anejo: Aged for one year or more, anejo is a much milder, softer, rounder tequila. If you're going to sip tequila straight, order an anejo.

Source: Bill Thompson, Executive Vice President of Brand Development for Sidney Frank Importing. For more about tequila, check out www.corazontequila.com.

THE BODY SHOT

If you need an excuse to lick someone in public, this is the best there is. Follow these seven steps to performing the perfect tequila body shot.

Step 1: Find a hot guy who's willing to bare a few inches of skin and be your body shot partner.

Step 2: Order two shots of tequila with two lime wedges and two teaspoons of sugar.

Step 3: Lick a spot on your partner's body (to make it sticky) and sprinkle sugar on it. Then he should do the same to you.

Step 4: Hold the lime wedge between the thumb and index finger of your left hand.

Step 5: Use your right hand to down the shot.

Step 6: Suck on the lime immediately after.

Step 7: Lick the sugar off of your partner (this can take as long as you like).

The Cocktail: Frozen Blue Moon Margarita

Description A bit of blue curacao turns a standard frozen margarita into a space-age experience.

Ingredients

1 oz. blanco tequila
1 oz. triple sec
½ oz. blue curacao

2 oz. sweet and sour mix
Splash of fresh lime juice

Directions Blend all ingredients with a cup of crushed ice until smooth. Pour into a salt-rimmed margarita glass.

—recipe courtesy of Las Margaritas restaurant in New York, New York

The Cocktail: Jalapeño Margarita

Description A dream come true for fans of savory, spicy drinks like the Bloody Mary, this totally unique cocktail requires a little careful mixing to get it just right. Foodies will go nuts for it.

Ingredients

1 ½ oz. tequila
¾ oz. triple sec
½ oz. light beer (pilsner or lager)
½ a fresh jalapeño

1 lime
Soda water
2 oz. sour mix

Directions Cut the jalapeño into small slices and add to a tall glass. Squeeze the juice of ½ of a lime over the jalapeño, add a splash of soda water, then muddle to extract the pepper's oils. Fill the rest of the glass with ice and add tequila, triple sec, and beer. Fill with sour mix and then squeeze the other half of the lime on top.

—recipe courtesy of Oba! in Portland, Oregon

MATING CALLS

Be a Shameless Flirt

Tequila is legendary for loosening up tight tongues, but thinking of a great pickup line in the heat of the moment is never easy. Here are five flirtatious lines to drop in a margarita bar when you're feeling . . .

Sassy: "Could you bite into this jalapeño and tell me what's hotter—the pepper or me?"

Sweet: "Either I've had too much tequila or you're incredibly cute."

Straightforward: "I can't finish these hot, delicious nachos. Do you guys want any?"

Silly: "Why don't you pretend I'm a *piñata* and hit on me?"

Shy: "It took two margaritas for me to work up enough courage just to say hi to you. Then I had three more. So do you want to do a body shot?"

MANLY DRINK TO TRY: THE ONE WITH THE WORM

Mezcal, not tequila, is the type of booze that sometimes comes with a fermented critter floating at the bottom of the bottle. A close relative of tequila, it comes from the Mexican state of Oaxaca, and is made using several different types of agave plants (tequila can only be made from the blue agave). Most villages in Oaxaca make their own Mezcal by cooking agave hearts in underground ovens, mashing them with horse-drawn millstones, then fermenting the resulting liquid combined with water in wooden vats, and finally distilling the mixture in clay or copper stills. Only a few brands, most famously Monte Alban Mezcal, actually add the worm—which is totally sanitized and therefore harmless to your health (though still pretty gross). Mezcal has a smokier flavor than tequila and, overall, a tougher, rougher image. Order a shot of Mezcal from a Mexican bartender and you're likely to see a big, approving smile spread across his face.

The Cocktail: House Party Margaritas

Description This super easy recipe is for a pitcher (six servings) of mouthwatering, thirst-quenching margaritas. Make it for your friends on a Saturday afternoon and bask in their gratitude.

Ingredients

3 cups tequila

½ cup triple sec

½ gallon fresh lime juice

6 sprigs of mint

Directions Mix tequila, lime juice, and triple sec in a glass pitcher. Rim large glasses or paper cups with granulated sugar and kosher salt then fill cup with ice. Pour in margarita mixture and top with a fresh sprig of mint.

—recipe courtesy of the Ammo Cafe in Los Angeles, California

The Cocktail: Cloud Nine Margarita

Description Adding an egg to a margarita might sound strange, but it gives this cocktail a light, frothy, smooth feel and flavor that's truly fantastic. Try it and you'll be hooked.

Ingredients

2 oz. tequila

1 oz. triple sec

Juice of 1 medium orange

Splash of lime juice

1 egg with the yolk removed

Directions Add tequila, triple sec, freshly squeezed orange juice and splash of lime juice to an ice-filled cocktail shaker. Top with the white of one egg then shake very well. Strain into a martini glass.

—recipe courtesy of Las Margaritas restaurant in New York, New York

FIELD GUIDE TO GUYS

Species: El Romeo

Common Physical Traits: Longish hair, a five o'clock shadow, silk button-down shirt, black jeans, braided leather bracelet, long suede coat

Scent: Cuba Gold by Cuba

Animal Behavior: Stands with one arm resting on the bar while his dark eyes look piercingly around the room for a woman who looks like she wants to dance.

Natural Habitat: The Margarita Bar

Tips for the Romeo Hunter: Attract this predator by meeting his intense stare with a few bats of your eyelashes and tapping your feet to the music.

What You'll Get for Your Birthday: A trip to a little-known South American beach

JUNGLE SOUNDS

What's on the Jukebox in a Margarita Bar

Mariachi Vargas *Serie Platino: 20 Exitos* (BMG/U.S. Latin, 1997)
Mariachi Vargas has been hot since the 1930s (every time a member becomes too old to play, he is replaced by the top young talent in the country). This is the kind of big-band mariachi music that showed up in Hollywood films set in Mexico in the 1950s. Unstoppably upbeat and fun.

Control Machete *Artilleria Pesada Presente* (Uni/Polygram Latino, 1999)
The toughest band to ever come out of Mexico is probably best known for its hit single "Si Señor," which was featured in a Levi's commercial and included on the soundtrack of the film *Amores Perros.* Their sound is deep-throated urban rap with the kind of base that makes your lower body move by itself.

Paulina Rubio *Border Girl* (Universal, 2002)
She's to Mexico what Kylie Minogue is to Australia and Shakira is to Colombia—

the country's top female pop star. And like those other leading ladies, she's cheesy enough to make a block of cheddar jealous. But there's a time and a place for tacky pop music, and in a margarita bar doing tequila shots is one of the best.

Los Lobos *Kiko* (WEA/Warner Bros., 1992)
Yes, this is the band that recorded Richie Valens' "La Bamba," but they're anything but a one-hit wonder. Kiko is an experimental album that parlays traditional Latin sounds into fiery rock tunes and bluesy ballads. Dial it up on the jukebox for a pleasant surprise.

Alejandro Fernandez *Me Estoy Enamorando* (Sony Discos, 1997)
His dad was big-time ranchera star Vicente Fernandez, but the sexy Alejandro is now even more popular on the Mexican music scene. His voice is as smooth as the skin of a male model, and his pop ballads are moody and dramatic with plenty of gorgeous guitar flourishes. This album is his best to date.

The Cocktail: Jeffrey's Mandarita

Description Any cocktail that includes a cup of tangerine sorbet is going to trigger your brain's pleasure centers. Not surprisingly, this is the most popular drink at Jeffrey's.

Ingredients

2 oz. tequila
1 oz. Cointreau
Juice of ½ of a lime

1 cup tangerine sorbet
2 slices of lime

Directions This recipe makes enough for two. Combine all ingredients except for the lime slices in a blender and blend until slushy. Serve in large martini glasses and garnish with lime slices.

—recipe courtesy of Jeffrey's in Austin, Texas

The Cocktail: Dos Caminos Strawberry Margarita

Description From one of the best Mexican spots in New York City comes this updated version of a vacation classic. You'll love its delicate strawberry flavor and hint of mint.

Ingredients

2 oz. reposado tequila

4 to 6 fresh strawberries

4 to 6 fresh mint leaves

Splash of lime juice

Splash of simple syrup

Directions Muddle strawberries and mint together with a couple of ice cubes. Add tequila, lime juice and simple syrup, then shake with ice and strain into an ice-filled rocks glass. Garnish with a mint leaf.

—recipe courtesy of Dos Caminos in New York, New York

JUNGLE MOVES

Chicks and Salsa

You can shake your butt to Latin music just about anywhere, but if you want to get into a serious groove while sipping a sumptuous cocktail, head to the margarita bar's distant cousin: the salsa club.

Salsa isn't one of those activities you can just pick up by watching. You need to take a few lessons to learn how to shake your booty in classic Afro-Cuban style. But once you've got the basics down, this passionate dance will become one of your favorite nightlife pastimes. Here are some inside tips on salsa clubbing from Rodney Lopez, a professional dancer, salsa club regular, and instructor at New York's Dance Manhattan.

Take group and private lessons

The group experience will get you used to dancing with a lot of different partners at different skill levels, which is what you'll encounter out at a club.

But taking a private lesson once in a while will give you the individual attention you need to become a fantastic dancer.

Make yourself visible
If you're out at a club and you want to be asked to dance, stand close to the dance floor and do the basic step while standing in place to let guys know you're ready to go.

Be a good partner
"Don't be a diva," says Lopez. Smile and make occasional eye contact when you're dancing, and never walk away from your partner in the middle of a song—unless he's being rude or too rough. If you don't want to dance with someone again, say "thank you" when the music stops and walk away.

Follow the leader
In partner dancing, it's just as hard to be a good follower as it is to be a good lead. The trick is not to try to anticipate your partner's movements, but rather to stay alert and just react to what his body is telling you.

Don't let the sexiness turn you off
"Like so many other Latin dances, salsa has a very sensual image, but the passion is really for the music and the dance," says Lopez. Traditional salsa dancing requires that you stay a respectful distance apart. If a guy is getting too close, use your left hand to firmly push his right shoulder further away from your body.

Say yes
You'll have the most fun at a salsa club if you're open-minded about who you dance with. "A salsa dance is like a polite but lively conversation between strangers," says Lopez. "The more people you interact with, the more of a dynamic good time you're going to have." And keep your eyes out for dancin' grampas who will probably be able to spin you around with more panache than three younger guys put together.

Una Cerveza, Por Favor

Not sure which Mexican beer will please your picky palate? Maybe this will help.

If you like light, refreshing pilsners that make it easy to drink two or three in a row, try Corona, Pacifico, or Sol.

If you like medium-bodied beers that have more malt flavor, try Carta Blanca, Dos Equis Special, or Bohemia.

If you like full-bodied brews that coat your tongue and taste like licking a stalk of wheat, try Dos Equis Amber or Negro Modelo.

JUNGLE LOOKS

What to wear to a Margarita Bar

The Pretty Peasant: Delicate peasant shirts were all the rage last spring, so dig one of them out of your closet and wear it with a pair of soft old jeans to look laid-back but very feminine.

The Laura Ingalls Wilder: It's the look that makes city boys wish they lived in a little house on the prairie—a floral sundress paired with cowboy boots. Too cold for a sundress? Warm it up with a denim jacket and a pair of textured knit tights.

The Sexy Cowgirl: A teeny denim miniskirt (so what if you couldn't possibly ride a horse in it?), topped with a fitted, Western shirt that's unbuttoned just enough to reveal a millimeter of cleavage. And cowboy boots, of course.

The Updated Frida: For an artsy, but still urban look, wear a long, frilly, colorful peasant skirt with a fitted, plain white T-shirt. Add an eye-catching silver and turquoise choker or a brown leather wristband.

JUNGLE TALES

The Tequila Made Me Do It

"Two friends and I were on a road trip through California when we passed this enormous bar called Buck's Crazy Horse Saloon in Chico, CA. We weren't going to go in, but then we saw a sign that said there was a mechanical bull inside. We were all fans of the movie *Urban Cowboy* and were *not* going to miss this opportunity to make like Debra Winger. After many margaritas we got up the guts to get in line for a ride, and by the time it was our turn everyone in the bar was crowded around watching. None of the three of us even rode a bike, much less a horse or a bull, but my friend Kathy got up there first and after five seconds, went sliding off the side into a pile of straw. Jen went second and did the exact same thing. I almost backed out but ended up sitting on the bull and waiting for it to start. It began moving really slowly and I held on, no problem. The bull operator made the thing buck and turn faster but still I held on, even though my head was spinning. Then he turned it up one more notch and I felt my body lift off the saddle and the next thing I knew I was on the floor—with no shirt on. My blouse had caught on the stirrup and been completely torn off." —Danielle, 32

JUNGLE PARTY

How to Throw a Friggin' Fiesta

Drink Menu

Margaritas have just three basic ingredients—tequila, triple sec, and lime juice—so getting ready for a Mexican-themed fete isn't very hard in the liquor department. The only decisions you need to make are what brands to buy and which extra ingredients you need to make specialty versions of the cocktail. If you want extra smooth libations, drop a little more cash on a few bottles of reposado tequila. But it isn't really necessary. Most bartenders use less expensive blanco tequila because the lime juice does a good enough job of taking the edge off. It's your choice. Triple sec is a strong, clear, orange-flavored liqueur. You can either buy an inexpensive brand, like De Kuyper Triple Sec, or you can opt for pricier triples secs, the most popular of which are Cointreau and Grand Marnier. As with tequila, it won't make much of a difference to anyone but the most diehard connoisseurs. A fantastic trio would be the Dos Caminos Strawberry Margarita (light and sweet), the Cloud Nine Margarita (the classic with a gourmet twist), and the Jeffrey's Mandarita (a grown-up slushy). For those, you'll need to pick up limes, strawberries, mint, tangerine sorbet, and eggs.

Glassware and Garnish
Margarita glasses are truly optional, and given that they're only good for one cocktail, there's no reason to go out and buy a bunch of them. You can serve all ice-less margaritas in martini glasses and the frozen kind can be poured into tall highball glasses, or rocks glasses, or paper cups for that matter. The glasses are best garnished by moistening the rim with a lime wedge and then dipping the cup upside down on a glass of powdered sugar or kosher salt, depending on what the recipe calls for. Or just cut a wheel-shaped slice of lime and stick it on the edge of the glass.

Decorations
Your apartment is only a few red-white-and-green garlands away from looking like a Mexican village on the 5th of May. Drape paper streamers all along the ceiling, hang sombreros on the walls, and let a loud, colorful *piñata* or two swing above your guests' heads. Don't be afraid of overdoing it. For environmental authenticity, consider picking up an oversized cactus from Home Depot and using it as a centerpiece. Offer your guy friends stick-on handlebar moustaches as they walk in the door and tell your girlfriends to wear cowboy hats. Sunflowers are traditional

Mexican flowers that are easy to come by. Buy a bunch and put individual blooms in bud vases on windowsills and in the bathroom.

Lighting

With all those paper decorations around, candles probably aren't a good idea. Instead, hang tiny white, green and/or red Christmas lights—or even better, chili pepper lights—to give the party a warm glow.

Audio and Visuals

Play movies (with the mute button on) that feature men in tight pants and big sombreros like *The Three Amigos* (1986) or *The Mask of Zorro* (1998); great westerns like *The Good, The Bad and The Ugly* (1966); or the eye-popping, jaw-dropping Mexican road trip flick *Y Tu Mama Tambien* (2001). Fill your CD changer with traditional Mexican music by bands like Mariachi Vargas, or opt for a more modern selection of tunes by playing the two-CD *Amores Perros* soundtrack.

Buy fiesta supplies online at:
www.partyadventure.com
www.thepinatastore.com
www.cheesylights.com

MISS MIXOLOGIST

Female bartenders confess what they love best about being behind the bar.

"Cocktails are my passion. I think women make wonderful bartenders because we like to take care of people. We're more attentive to others' needs. I'll say hello to someone who walks into the bar and try to sense what kind of a day they're having. And I really do want to make them the perfect cocktail—the one that's going to turn their day around, perk them up, and make them feel like a fun night has started. A great cocktail—well balanced, made with fresh ingredients, and very well shaken—can change a person's perspective in a single sip." —Audrey Saunders, mixologist at Bemelman's Bar at The Carlyle Hotel in New York, New York

"I love the fact that people come here to have a good time and that I'm part of the reason they're having a good time. Everyone loves to meet new people and have new experiences, so I introduce people to each other all the time. By the end of the night one end of the bar is talking to the other end of the bar. Another reason I like bartending is because the people I work with are like a family. In a job like this, you just be yourself and everyone gets to know the real you. You don't have to wear a suit or keep your personality in check. The friendships you develop aren't just 'work friendships,' they're closer than that." —Tarren Geddes, bartender at Purple Martini in Denver, Colorado

"Bartending has brought a lot into my life, including more self-confidence. It's helped me overcome a lot of fears. Everyone has a wild side, but sometimes you're afraid to let it out. Working at Coyote Ugly lets me be my craziest self. I wake up in the morning and wait all day long to go to work. I love putting on a show for my customers and making them laugh. I used to be outgoing to a point, but not as much as I became when I got behind the bar. It's exhilarating." — Tara Jenneman, bartender at Coyote Ugly in New Orleans, Louisiana

"Bartending is a great way to make money while pursuing other things. Your days are free and you can have up to four days off, while still making the same amount of money as your 9 to 5 friends. At times it can be stressful and there are always difficult people that you have to deal with, but if you're fortunate enough to work with a fun staff and a good clientele, it usually feels more like a party than a job." —Liz Green, bartender at Light in New York, New York

"I love the bar I work at because it's a place where women can come to let loose. We have dozens of bras hanging over the bar, and it is not uncommon to see women lying across the bar getting salt licked off their bellies. We have outrageous bachelorette parties. Women also come here to troll for men. It is pretty much a sausage-fest. The ratio is definitely in the favor of women." —Jory Jackson, bartender at Dick's Last Resort in San Diego, California

The Karaoke Bar

It's always surprising when something that's been undeniably dorky for years suddenly loses its stigma. It happened with tennis (Venus, Serena, and Anna heated things up), velour sweatsuits (thank J. Lo's clothing line for that), and nerdy fantasy flicks (who didn't like *The Lord of the Rings*?).

So has karaoke earned a spot on that list? In at least one instance, yes. The coolest karaoke out there involves screaming punk or heavy metal lyrics to a roomful of moshing rock-worshippers while a live band goes ballistic behind you. It's wild, exhilarating, gritty, ballsy, and if you haven't seen it yet you're in for an I-can't-believe-it's-cool surprise.

Not that cool matters, because we don't go to karaoke bars to exert our hipness, we go to have a goofy, un-self-conscious good time. You can't be serious every day of your life, right? Hell, no. So grab a few friends, head down to Chung Lee's Dumpling Hut & Karaoke Palace (or whatever your local karaoke joint is called) and belt out lines like: "I went to a party last Saturday night / I didn't get laid, I got in a fight / Uhhhh-huuuuh / It ain't no big thing . . . " You'll have a blast being Lita Ford for a few short minutes and the crowd will adore you.

Like so many other destinations in the Cocktail Jungle, karaoke presents yet another way to loosen up and let go. No matter what you feel like getting off of your chest, there's a song that can help you do it. Desperate for some time off from work? Sing "Vacation" by The Go-Go's. Got a mad crush on a hard-to-get guy? Blondie's "The Tide Is High" is a perfect fit. Just feel like making a lot of noise? Scream something by The Sex Pistols. And don't be nervous about screwing up, because everyone screws up. Which is what makes watching karaoke as fun as doing it. There's nothing like witnessing a couple of your friends on stage trying to pass for Salt 'n' Pepa and not even coming close.

Where did karaoke come from? It all started in Japan when stressed-out businessmen started singing at bars after work to shake off their uptight daytime demeanors (who knows where *they* got the idea). From there it spread throughout Asia and eventually made it to the United States. Now you can choose from three totally different kinds of karaoke. You can opt for the original kind in a barely lit Asian lounge where the karaoke machine is set in front of the room and people take turns singing to a well-behaved audience. Or, if you'd rather not embarrass yourself in front of strangers, there are karaoke clubs that offer private rooms with soundproof doors. Only the bartender will pop in from time to time to refill your drinks. And finally there's live-band karaoke like the kind that happens on Monday nights at Arlene's Grocery in New York, New York. This is the punk/heavy metal version, and there's nothing well-behaved about it. The singer and band are on a raised platform in a room that's usually used for concerts. The crowd is big and loud and unafraid to boo someone off the stage. It takes guts to get up there and sing, but the payoff is huge, because for as long as the song lasts, you'll feel 100% like a rock star.

The Cocktail: Sake Mai Tai

Description Tropical Mai Tais are famous for packing a powerful punch. This Japanese version is lighter and more refreshing, but just as effective.

Ingredients

2 oz. sake
1 oz. pineapple juice
1 oz. orange juice

¼ oz. grenadine
½ oz. rum

Directions Pour all ingredients in a highball glass over ice. Garnish with an orange and a cherry.

—recipe courtesy of Ozumo in San Francisco, California

The Cocktail: Plum Martini

Description If you like your cocktails delicate and sweet, you'll love this sake bar special.

Ingredients
2 oz. sake
2 oz. plum wine

Directions Shake sake and wine with ice and strain into a martini glass.
—recipe courtesy of Yoshi's in Oakland, California

JUNGLE BASICS

Sake 101

Sake is a 6,800-year-old alcoholic beverage made from four main ingredients: rice, water, yeast, and koji, an enzyme used in fermentation. The way sake is made is similar to beer, but the ancient spirit is served and sipped like wine. Though it was the Japanese who refined it and made it popular worldwide, a rougher form of sake was first invented in China. Sake is served chilled or hot depending on its quality. As a rule, the good stuff is served cold and the bad is heated. Like beer, sake is best when fresh. There's no such thing as "aged sake."

Sake's image is very Californian. There are only six sake breweries (a.k.a. sakeries) in the U.S. and five of them are in California. Like sushi, sake has a reputation for being fresh and healthy. It doesn't contain sulfites, has little acidity, and because of its relatively low alcohol content, you have to drink a lot of it to end up with a hangover. Clear and crisp, sake is great for mixing, and sake-based creations are just starting to show up on cocktail menus at trendy drinking spots across the country. Of course, Japanese restaurants and karaoke bars are highly likely to have sake on hand.

There are many different ways of categorizing sake, but the two you need to know about are Ginjo (premium) and Daiginjo (ultra-premium). Ginjo sake is smooth and refined (rice kernels are milled to less than 60% of their original size). Ginjo has a mild, clean taste. Daiginjo sake is even more refined (rice kernels are milled to less than 50% of their original size), and has more complex flavors and a stronger aroma. Both are served chilled. Following in the footsteps of vodka, infused sake is the latest development. Pear, raspberry, ginger, plum, and hazelnut flavored sake are now available from major sake brands like Hakusan, SakeOne, and YSake.

Source: www.sakeone.com

The Cocktail: Mango Mojito

Description Add mango to just about anything and you're going to get something golden, fruity, and smooth. Add it to a mojito and you get solid gold in a glass.

Ingredients

¼ fresh mango, cut into small pieces
3 or 4 sprigs of fresh mint
4 oz. sake

1 oz. triple sec
½ of a fresh lime
Soda water

Directions Muddle mango and mint with ¼ glass of ice. Add sake, triple sec, and fresh-squeezed lime juice. Add more ice, shake, and strain into a rocks glass over ice. Top with a splash of soda and garnish with mint.

—recipe courtesy of Blowfish Sushi in San Francisco, California

MATING CALLS

Get a Guy's Attention in a Karaoke Bar

Feed His Ego: Approach him right after he sings and say "That was so good my friend and I want to buy you a drink. So what'll it be?"

Hit Him Over the Head: Sing "Damn, I Wish I Was Your Lover" by Sophie B. Hawkins or "Let's Get It On" by Marvin Gaye while throwing furtive glances in his direction.

Tempt Him With S&M: Stroll up to a group of guys and ask "Excuse me, will one of you be free in about five minutes? I'm looking for someone to help me act out 'Whip It' by Devo."

Seduce Him Subliminally: Send a man's mind careening to gutter by saying something "innocent" like "I'm a karaoke virgin, do you do it all the time?"

Beg Him to Do a Duet: Say you're dying to sing "Don't You Want Me?" by Human League and need a man ASAP.

The Cocktail: Cucumber Cooler

Description This number will bring your body temperature down after you've been basking in the spotlight.

Ingredients

4 thin slices of cucumber   1 oz. simple syrup

4 oz. of sake   Soda water

Juice of ½ lime

Directions Muddle cucumber in a rocks glass with ¼ glass of ice. Add more ice, sake, lime juice, and simple syrup. Top with soda water, stir, and garnish with a cucumber slice.

—recipe courtesy of Blowfish Sushi in San Francisco, California

FIELD GUIDE TO GUYS

Species: The Broker

Common Physical Traits: Pleated khaki pants, Brooks Brothers dress shirt, navy blue blazer, Nautica watch, neat haircut, laptop bag, super hi-tech cell phone

Scent: Cool Water by Davidoff or anything by Hugo Boss

Animal Behavior: Straightforward and confident, he'll introduce himself and ask if he can buy you a drink.

Natural Habitat: The Karaoke Bar

Tips for the Broker Hunter: Good old feminine flirting will knock this guy's Banana Republic cashmere socks off, so flip your hair, make lingering eye contact, and swing your hips while walking by his table.

What You'll Get for Your Birthday: Lingerie and a robe from Victoria's Secret

JUNGLE SOUNDS

The Top 10 Karaoke Tunes

Make it easy on yourself and pick a few tunes off of this list of karaoke favorites. They all have simple melodies and lyrics that are damn near impossible to forget. "And if you're a woman over the age of 25, you already know them by heart," says New York's punk rock/heavy metal karaoke expert Rob Kemp.

"We Got the Beat" by The Go-Go's
"Shena Is a Punk Rocker" by The Ramones
"You Give Love a Bad Name" by Bon Jovi
"Paradise City" by Guns 'n' Roses
"I Love Rock 'n' Roll" by Joan Jett
"Whole Lotta Love" by Led Zeppelin
"Kiss Me Deadly" by Lita Ford
"Hit Me With Your Best Shot" by Pat Benetar
"Talk Dirty to Me" by Poison
"Eighteen and Life" by Skid Row
"Hot for Teacher" by Van Halen

BAR FENG SHUI

Feng Shui Tips for Barflies

Luck isn't exactly scientific, but trying these ancient party tricks couldn't hurt!

Sit in the Feng Shui Power Position Face the door with a full view of the room.

Stash a Crystal in Your Purse Crystals harness *chi*, the feel-good energy that brings good things your way. Pull it out when you're bored and watch the light split into colors.

Practice Name Dropping Feng Shui practitioners place pictures of famous people in their homes to boost their reputation. Mentioning the names of famous/important people whom you know is the next best thing when you're out on the town.

Get Things in Twos To attract a hot new man into your life, get into the habit of pulling two napkins off of the pile, ordering two cherries in your cocktail, wearing two bracelets on your wrist, putting two candles on your table.

Pick a Lounge That Feels Alive If you're feeling blah, trickling waterfalls, fresh-smelling plants, and soothing music will lift your spirits.

Streamline Your Stuff Clutter is a Feng Shui no-no. Dump whatever you don't need out of your wallet and bag (except that crystal, of course) and only keep what's absolutely essential. You'll feel lighter, freer, and more at ease.

The Cocktail: Reformed USSR

Description Creamy and dreamy, this drink got its name because it looks white as snow and tastes so new and delicious, it's downright revolutionary.

Ingredients

1 ½ oz. sake	½ oz. white creme de cacao
1 oz. vodka	2 oz. half and half

Directions Shake with ice and strain into a large martini glass.

—recipe courtesy of Anzu in San Francisco, California

The Cocktail: Ginger Martini

Description A gourmet cocktail for ginger fans. It's perfect as an après-sushi, pre-karaoke treat.

Ingredients
3 oz. sake
1 oz. ginger brandy
½ oz. peach schnapps

Directions Shake with ice and strain into a martini glass.
—recipe courtesy of RA Sushi in Scottsdale, Arizona

JUNGLE MOVES

Classic Karaoke Tips

The music is coming from speakers, the lyrics are flashing across a screen, and the crowd is chatting, laughing, and sipping lychee martinis. Yes, it's a low-key scene, but that doesn't mean it isn't nerve-wracking. Use these tips to calmly and confidently ace your debut.

1. Try to imagine that you're singing to just one person, someone who thinks everything you do is out-of-this-world amazing—like your grandmother.
2. Don't look directly at the faces in the crowd. Instead look just over their heads. They won't know the difference and you'll feel less nervous.
3. Don't worry about whether or not you sound good, just put as

much inflection into your voice as possible, like the way you would if you were reading out loud to a child.

4. Be yourself: You'll have more fun if you stick with what feels natural. So if you have a big personality and love to be over-the-top, pick a disco tune, dance like Dee-Lite, and belt out lyrics like a drag-queen on speed. If you're normally shy and reserved, select a low-key song, sit on a stool, put both hands on the microphone, and sing like Lisa Loeb.

5. Breathe normally into your stomach. Taking in or breathing out too much air will make it harder for you to sing.

Source: Jocelyn Rasmussen, a singing teacher in New York, New York (www.morethansinging.com)

Live Punk and Heavy Metal Karaoke Tips

A live band is behind you, a sea of screaming fans is in front of you, and you have to sing without a cheatsheet. Here's how to blow the crowd away, baby.

1. Practice at home by dancing and singing along to a CD in front of the mirror. You'll feel like an idiot while doing it, but when you're on stage you'll be so grateful that you did.

2. Don't stress about what your voice sounds like—as long as you put out a lot of energy, you'll win the audience over—but do make sure you know exactly when you're supposed to start and stop singing.

3. Be crazy. Throw beer. Shake your booty. Headbang. Jump up and down. Make a scene. Only the lazy and boring get booed.

4. Get tipsy enough to feel relaxed and confident, but don't get so drunk that you'll start slurring words or fall off the stage.

Source: Rob Kemp, punk rock/heavy metal karaoke bassist in New York, New York (www.punkmetalkaraoke.com)

The Cocktail: Lychee Martini

Description A small Asian fruit with sweet white flesh, a lychee tastes like a cross between a pear and a grape. If you order one drink at a karaoke bar, make it this one.

Ingredients

2 oz. vodka

1 tsp. lychee juice

1 lychee peeled and pitted

Directions Shake vodka and lychee juice with ice and strain into a martini glass. Spear the lychee on a toothpick and drop into the glass.

—recipe courtesy of Congee Village in New York, New York

The Cocktail: Yokozuna

Description A "Yokozuna" is a high-ranking sumo wrestler, but there's nothing heavy about this cocktail—the grapefruit juice keeps it light and tart.

Ingredients

2 oz. sake

½ oz. triple sec

½ oz. freshly squeezed grapefruit juice

Directions Shake with ice and strain into a martini glass.

—recipe courtesy of Ozumo in San Francisco, California

JUNGLE LOOKS

What to Wear to a Karaoke Bar

The average rock star is 75% style and 25% talent. Don the look of an MTV diva and you're already more than halfway there.

Private School Punk: To look like a true British punk, pair a plaid miniskirt with a white button-down shirt, fishnets, and combat boots. Smudge on plenty of thick black eyeliner, sneer like Billy Idol, and sing something by Adam Ant.

Pop Princess: Dress like you just graduated from Malibu High—little pastel baby-tees with "sexy" written across the chest in gold sequins, skintight jeans, and white leather high-heeled boots. Sing something sugary sweet like "Two of Hearts" by Stacey Q.

R&B Diva: Get decked out in head-to-toe leather to look and feel like Mary J. Blige. Add big hoop earrings, long glittery nails, and a ton of attitude. Pick your favorite Eve or Lil' Kim song, just leave out the X-rated lyrics.

Sophisticated Songstress: Ladies like Celine Dion and Faith Hill prefer flowy, feminine outfits to flash. A silk ruffled blouse and a pair of fitted, black satin pants will look perfectly appropriate while you're crooning the theme song to *Titanic*.

Grunge Girlie: If you'd rather sing Pearl Jam than Pink, there's no reason to go glam. A wife-beater tank top, ripped jeans, and old sneakers are sexy in their own garage-goddess kind of way.

JUNGLE TALES

Full Karaoke Exposure

"A coworker and I wanted to try karaoke but were totally embarrassed to sing in front of other people, so we went to a bar in a part of town where no one we know hangs out. The place was really dark and mostly empty so we hogged the machine and sang all these horrible songs. We did almost the entire *Grease* soundtrack and my friend even sang a few from *The Sound of Music*. We made asses out of ourselves but had a great time. The next day we walked into work and heard the sound of our cracking voices coming from the conference room. A guy we worked with had been in the audience because he lives around the corner from the bar and hangs out there all the time. When he saw that it was us bleating into the microphone, he ran home to get his MP3 player and recorded the whole thing. We never, ever lived it down." Karina, 27.

JUNGLE PARTY

How to Host a Karaoke and Cocktails Party

Drink Menu

Sake-based cocktails are a sexy twist that'll help give your karaoke party more of a nightclub atmosphere. A delicious lychee martini should be first on your menu since they're always a huge hit. Whoever doesn't happen to like the sweet lychee martini will love the Yokozuna because of its tartness. A good third is the Cucumber Cooler—totally unique, light and refreshing. And to finish off your list, the Reformed USSR makes a decadent late-night concoction/dessert. You'll need a good-quality, versatile sake to mix drinks with like Y Sake Wind, a dry Daiginjo with a hint of a melon/cantaloupe/mango flavor and a clean finish, or Momokawa Silver Sake, which has a slight green apple aroma and makes a good substitute for vodka.

Glassware and Garnish

The above cocktails require only two types of glasses: martini and rocks. For garnish you'll need lychees and cucumbers. Buy canned or jarred lychees that are packed in their natural juices and use the juice to mix with sake and create your martini.

Decorations

It will only take a few Japanese touches to make your living room feel like a karaoke lounge. Lucky bamboo plants—you've seen these tall leafy stalks everywhere—are inexpensive, beautiful, and easy to care for once the party is over. Place three or four of them in a tall glass vase in the center of the room. A couple of silver and orange goldfish in an elegant bowl are another great idea for live Asian decor. (If you don't want to keep them forever, give them away at the end of the night.) Less permanent are Japanese paper decorations in the shape of fish, kimonos, dragons, and/or parasols. You'll need at least one Lucky Cat—a Feng Shui symbol that no Asian restaurant goes without, it's a white, wide-eyed porcelain statue of a cat that sits up tall and holds one arm up in the air. It's believed to bring good fortune (in the form of lots of cash) to any room in which it is placed.

Lighting

Use all-white candles or a few Japanese paper lanterns to give your pad a flattering glow. Just make sure there's at least one light source that you can use like a spotlight on the singer.

Audio and Visuals

You don't need a karaoke machine, but they are easy enough to rent. A quick Internet or phonebook search under karaoke will dig up a few options. They cost anywhere from $50 to $150 a night. Another option is to just buy a handful of karaoke CDs and play them in your stereo while a guest sings along sans microphone. In either case you'll probably need to print out all the song lyrics on sheets of paper unless the karaoke company does that for you.

Two great DVDs to rent and play in the background are *Duets* (2000), a flick starring Gwyneth Paltrow and Huey Lewis that's all about, you guessed it, karaoke. And *My Best Friend's Wedding* (1997), for the scene where Cameron Diaz trumps Julia Roberts by bringing down the karaoke house in spite of her horrendous voice. Hey, if Gwyneth and Cameron can do karaoke and still be cool, so can the rest of us.

Buy karaoke CDs and Asian party supplies online at:
www.karaoke.com
www.japaneseteaparties.com
www.garden-gifts.com

GOING TO A BAR ALONE

Snag these secrets from girls who know how to enjoy a drink solo.

Be a Regular
"I wouldn't go to just any bar by myself, but there's one place where I hang out all the time with my friends so I feel really comfortable there. It's an Irish pub with a great jukebox and a popcorn machine. If no one is up for going out on a Thursday night, I'll just pop in for a beer, play my favorite Stones songs, and chow down on popcorn." —Debbie, 29

Get Into the Game
"I go to sports bars, sit somewhere with a good view of the screen, and just watch whatever is on." —Katherine, 27

Flash a Smile
"My best friend is constantly showing up late to bars so I find myself sitting there alone all the time. But you wouldn't believe how many people I've met that way. All you have to do is smile at whomever happens to be sitting around you and if they feel like saying hi, they will." —Sarah, 23

Get Organized
"I'll sit at a table in a quiet lounge and get totally organized. I'll order a mojito then write out a to-do list, enter numbers into my Palm Pilot, jot down notes about something I'm working on, or make phone calls. It's a lot nicer to get all that done in a candlelit room with soft jazz playing than sitting home at my kitchen table." —Lindsey, 33

Hit a Hotel Bar

"Hotel bars are best when you're out on your own. They tend to be less busy and the bartenders are usually these charismatic older guys who are used to yapping with execs on business trips. The second you sit down they come over and ask you how you are. Ask them a few questions back and that's all it takes—they'll chat your ear off for as long as you want to listen. If there are other people alone at the bar, a good bartender will bring them into the conversation, too." —Pam, 31

Be a Pinball Wizard

"If you've never played pinball before you have no idea how fun it can be. One bar I love to pop into when I'm walking home from work has five machines and I just feed them quarters and keep myself entertained. It makes so much noise, cute guys are always coming over to see what my score is." —Tanya, 21

See Live Music

"If I feel like going out and everyone is busy I'll go to a bar that has live music. You don't feel awkward because all you have to do is sit or stand there and watch the band like everyone else. " —Neko, 24

Bring a Good Book

"My favorite thing to do on a Sunday afternoon is to go to this cute place near my apartment, sit by the window and read a magazine, a book, or write in my journal, while sipping a beer. If I don't feel like reading or writing I'll just gaze out the window at whomever is walking by." —Lisa, 29

The Five Star Hotel Bar

The dimly lit velvet and leather upholstered lounges of classic, luxury hotels are by far the most underrated nightlife destinations in a hipster's Rolodex of hotspots. Luckily, it's the very buzz that they lack that makes them so fantastic. Quiet except for the hushed sounds of jazz and the soft whispers of couples and corporate giants tucked away in corners, the best hotel bars make you feel as sexy and mysterious as the lead babe in a Bond film.

Not to be confused with such ultramodern hotel watering holes as those designed by Ian Schrager or those found at W's all over the country, the cocktail room at a grand old hotel is a totally different animal. Instead of seeing and being seen, patrons disappear into plush booths and soft shadows to negotiate confidential business deals or pursue inappropriate romantic affairs. Discreet waiters and waitresses provide the kind of subtle yet attentive service you'd expect from a seasoned butler. Which is only natural since every employee here is used to catering to the very rich, the very powerful, and the very, very picky. As long as you're well-dressed and well-behaved, they'll assume you're one of the above.

Even more enjoyable than the pampering wait staff are the exceptional cocktails. Unlike other bars that select bartenders based on who has the prettiest face and the perkiest cleavage, hotel bars are famous for featuring older mixologists with several years—if not several decades—of experience. These liquor wizards have tinkered with hundreds of classic recipes until they get them exactly right, so here's your chance to order a Sidecar, a Pink Lady, or a Champagne Cocktail, without worrying about whether or not the bartender knows how to make them. And smaller crowds mean they have more time to squeeze fresh fruit juices and properly shake cocktails until they're adequately chilled and have the perfect ratio of water to booze—little details that mean the difference between a truly fabulous treat and just another drink down the hatch.

For the ultimate experience, avoid all chain hotels but the most posh and sophisticated. Think The Ritz or The Four Seasons. Smaller hotels with a glamorous past that still lure celebrity clientele—like The Carlyle Hotel in New York City and The Beverly Hills Hotel in Los Angeles—are ideal. The more steeped in rumors and legends, the better. Bring your dates for a heavy dose of old-fashioned romance or take your friends for a night of naughty gossip in a sultry setting. Oh, and about those corporate giants tucked away in corners—they often turn out to be young, handsome, single, and completely surprised to spot a stunning hottie like yourself in such an old-school atmosphere.

The Cocktail: Whiskey Smash/Mint Julep

Description Think you don't like whiskey? Try this refreshing concoction and you'll change your mind. The mint and lemon tame the bourbon until it purrs like a kitten. Leave out the lemon and it's a Mint Julep.

Ingredients
2 oz. bourbon
1 oz. simple syrup
3 fresh lemon wedges cut in half (for easier muddling)
1 sprig (approx. 6–10 leaves) of fresh mint

Directions Muddle lemon, simple syrup, and mint well. Add bourbon and shake well with ice. Strain into a rocks glass over ice. Garnish with mint leaves.

—recipe courtesy of Bemelman's Bar at The Carlyle Hotel in New York, New York

The Cocktail: Sidecar

Description When made with quality ingredients, the very classic sidecar is tart yet smooth. Request/use French Cognac and Cointreau for the best results. (Legend has it was named after a WWI captain who showed up at a bar in the sidecar of a chauffeur-driven motorcycle.)

Ingredients
1 ½ oz. brandy
¾ oz. triple sec
½ oz. fresh lemon juice

Directions Shake all ingredients with ice and strain into a chilled martini glass. Drop a twist of lemon in the drink to finish.
—recipe courtesy of The Bristol Lounge at The Four Seasons Hotel in Boston, Massachusetts

JUNGLE BASICS

The Anatomy of a Martini

A quick lesson on the most popular—and sexiest—libation of all time.

Drinking a martini is like dating a male model. Yeah, maybe you get to know him and he turns out to have plenty of fantastic inner qualities, but it's his chiseled good looks and sleek frame that lure you in. In his research, Lowell Edmunds, a classics professor at Rutgers University and author of *Martini, Straight Up,* discovered that the original triangular cocktail invented sometime in the late 1800s now has an image that's urbane, upscale, and very male. Maybe that explains why it's so much fun to have one in the palm of your hand.

The traditional components of a martini are gin and vermouth, but some time in the 1980s scenesters started requesting vodka martinis—probably because high-concept vodka marketing campaigns made it a more stylish choice. But all the Hollywood and literary glory associated with martinis refers to the one made with gin. At a reputable hotel bar, you'll probably still be served the authentic version—but it's always good to ask for a "gin martini" just to be sure. Here's what you'll usually get when you order your martini . . .

Traditional martini: (2-to-1 ratio) 2 oz. gin and 1 oz. dry vermouth

Dry: (5-to-1) 1 ⅔ oz. gin and ⅓ oz. dry vermouth

Extra dry: (8-to-1) 2 oz. gin and ¼ oz. dry vermouth

Sweet: 1 ½ oz. gin 1 ½ oz. sweet vermouth

Dirty: add 1 tsp. olive juice to any of the above

Extra dirty: add 2 tsp. olive juice to any of the above

You're not going to know which incarnation you like best until you try a few, so settle down with a quality bottle of gin and experiment a little. To make your own martini, add your preferred quantities of vermouth and gin to a mixing glass filled with ice and stir well but gently, then strain into a martini glass. Add a twist of lemon or an olive (or two if you like 'em).

When it's time to pick up your glass and drink, try lifting your elbow out to the side and wrapping your hand around the side of the glass that faces away from you. All of your fingers should be making contact with the body of the glass. This provides a secure yet graceful grip for those first few, precarious sips—just make sure you have plenty of elbow room.

The Cocktail: Champagne Cocktail

Description The ultimate spoiled starlet's drink, this is bubbly with a tasty, bittersweet kick. Of course, one won't be enough.

Ingredients

4–6 oz. well-chilled, dry champagne 2 dashes of bitters

1 cube of sugar

Directions Drop the cube into a chilled martini glass or champagne flute then splash bitters onto cube. Add champagne and a twist of lemon.

—recipe courtesy of The Greenhouse at The Ritz Carlton in Chicago, Illinois

The Cocktail: Matilda

Description You won't find this yummy citrus cocktail at any other bar because it was created in honor of Matilda, the Algonquin Hotel's famous orange cat.

Ingredients

2 oz. orange-infused vodka

Splash of triple sec

½ oz. champagne

Juice of 1 freshly squeezed orange

Directions Shake all ingredients except champagne with ice and strain into a martini glass. Float champagne and garnish with an orange twist.

—recipe courtesy of The Algonquin Hotel in New York, New York

MATING CALLS

Check-Out Time

Handsome hotel staffers are all too accustomed to flirting and being flirted with. Here's how to diss—or dish out—a killer come-on when the hottie involved is . . .

The Bellboy

To turn him down: "I'd love to, but the last thing I need is more relationship baggage."

To turn him on: "Would it be possible to see one of your rooms? Or should we just go to my place?"

The Bartender

To turn him down: "You'll do a better job of satisfying me if you stay behind the bar."

To turn him on: "I'd like the liquid equivalent of an orgasm . . . unless you're able to provide the real thing."

The Parking Valet
To turn him down: "No thanks, I have a funny feeling you've been in more girls than you have cars."
To turn him on: "Would you mind walking me to my car instead of driving it up? I don't want your boss to see me hit on you."

WHO IS DOROTHY PARKER?

The wittiest woman to ever walk into a hotel bar, poet and socialite Dorothy Parker was already penning theater reviews for *Vanity Fair* by the time she was 25. For a decade, she and several other literary luminaries like newspaperman Alexander Woollcott and *New Yorker* magazine founder Harold Ross would meet for lunch every day at The Algonquin Hotel in New York and gossip about everything and everyone who mattered. The luncheon became known as The Algonquin Round Table, and Parker's cutting observations and brilliant comebacks were frequently quoted in publications all over town. Steal a few of her most fabulous lines:

Dorothy on . . .
Martinis: "I like to have a martini, two at the very most. After three I'm under the table. After four I'm under the host."
Bimbos: "That woman speaks eighteen languages and she can't say 'no' in any of them."
Close quarters: "It's a small apartment—I barely have enough room to lay my hat and a few friends."
Katharine Hepburn: "She runs the gamut of emotions from A to B."
Prom: "If all the girls in attendance were laid end to end, I wouldn't be at all surprised."

Sex: "Ducking for apples—change one letter and it's the story of my life."
Seduction: "Brevity is the soul of lingerie."
Romance: "Love is like quicksilver in the hand. Leave the fingers open and it stays. Clutch it and it darts away."
Responsibility: "Take care of the luxuries and the necessities will take care of themselves."
Her own epitaph: "Excuse my dust."

BE A CIGAR AFICIONADA

Once upon a time, when you saw cigar smoke hovering in the air, you'd expect to find a George Burns look-alike puffing away at the source. But, along with cocktails, cigar smoking had a major revival in the '90s, with celebrities like Demi Moore, Gina Gershon, and Linda Evangelista appearing on the cover of *Cigar Aficionado* magazine. It wasn't uncommon to see fashionistas lighting up cigarillos outside of bars, or to spot a group of female execs walking into Club Macanudo on New York's Upper East Side for an after-work smoke. Since then, the hype may have faded, but the cigar smoking goes on—especially in upscale hotel bars. Have one after a satisfying meal and you'll understand what all the fuss is about—not to mention that you will finally have something in common with Fidel Castro.

Some tips for the new smoker:

1. When buying a cigar for the first time, go to a *bona fide* tobacco shop for the best experience. Confess to the tobacconist that you're a novice and ask for something mild and relatively small. You can also ask him or her to cut and light the cigar for you. A great first cigar to try is a CAO Gold Petite Corona Honey. CAO is the brand. Gold is the type. Petite Corona is the size. Honey is the flavor. If they don't have that, ask for a nice Macanudo or Cohiba.
2. Gently draw air through the head of the cigar into your mouth, and then slowly let the smoke drift back out. Never inhale.

3. Show off your ash. One sign of a quality cigar is that its ash will grow to a full inch or inch and a half without falling off. Wait until it's at least an inch long before tapping it ever so slightly against an ash tray.

4. In other countries, smoking a cigar with the band still on is tacky, but in the U.S. it's customary to smoke the cigar one-third of the way down and then remove it. If you try to take it off when the cigar is cold, you could damage the cigar's outer wrapper.

5. When you're finished smoking, don't stub out the cigar like you would a cigarette. Cigars naturally go out when you stop smoking them, so simply lay it in the ashtray and wait. You can re-light it when you're ready for more.

Source: Victoria McKee, spokesperson for General Cigar

The Cocktail: Pimm's Cup

Description Pepe DeArda, bartender at the always fabulous Polo Lounge for fourteen years, says the Pimm's was *the* celeb favorite in the '60s. It was named after Pimm's No. 1 liquor, a secret mix of gin, fruit juice, and spices.

Ingredients

2 oz. Pimm's No. 1 (or just use gin)   4–6 oz. ginger ale

1 oz. sweet and sour mix   1 cucumber slice

Directions Pour Pimm's (or gin) and sweet and sour mix over ice in a highball glass. Add ginger ale to fill. Stir well and garnish with a cucumber slice.

—recipe courtesy of The Polo Lounge at The Beverly Hills Hotel in Beverly Hills, California

The Cocktail: Old Cuban

Description This original cocktail by master mixologist Audrey Saunders is light, sweet, and uplifting. If you like mojitos, this will be your new favorite.

Ingredients

1 ½ oz. 8-year-old rum

1 oz. simple syrup

¾ oz. lime juice

2 oz. champagne

Dash of bitters

1 spring of mint (approx. 6–10 leaves)

Directions Muddle lime juice, simple syrup, mint, and bitters. Add rum and ice and shake well. Float champagne, stir twice, and garnish with mint leaves.

—recipe courtesy of Bemelman's Bar at The Carlyle Hotel in New York, New York

FIELD GUIDE TO GUYS

Species: The Up-and-Coming Tycoon

Common Physical Traits: Rolex watch, pinstripe Armani suit, refined leather briefcase, latest model Palm Pilot, close shave, salt-and-pepper hair

Scent: Cigar smoke and Safari cologne by Ralph Lauren

Animal Behavior: Sits at the bar and pretends to read *The Wall Street Journal* while scoping the room for beautiful women.

Natural Habitat: The Hotel Bar

Tips for the Tycoon Hunter: Appeal to his ever-expanding ego by complimenting him on his suit and asking him what kind of business he's in.

What You'll Get for Your Birthday: Diamond earrings

JUNGLE SOUNDS

The Piano Man

Though far more dynamic than a jukebox, the pianist in a hotel bar is just as good at taking requests—as long as you stick to the standards. Here's a list of slow to medium tempo tunes that any music man worth his salt will know, so go ahead and ask.

"Someone to Watch Over Me"
"Days of Wine and Roses"
"You Don't Know What Love Is"
"Like Someone in Love"
"Night and Day"
"Have You Met Miss Jones?"
"Prelude to a Kiss"
"Autumn in New York"
"Come Rain and Come Shine"
"Just Friends"
"Stella by Starlight"
"Moonlight in Vermont"
"April in Paris"
"There Will Never Be Another You"
"Autumn Leaves"
"There Is No Greater Love"

Tips on making your request: If the atmosphere in the bar is lively and the piano player talkative, wait until one song winds down and then call out the title of a song from your seat. On a quiet night, stroll up to the piano during an instrumental, wait for the pianist to acknowledge you then ask him if he knows the tune you're craving to hear.

The Cocktail: Gimlet

Description If martinis taste too strong for you, try a vodka or gin gimlet. They provide the same cheery sensation, but sharp lime juice and sugar make it easier to drink.

Ingredients

1 ½ oz. gin or vodka   1 tsp. sugar
1 oz. lime juice

Directions Pour ingredients into a rocks glass filled with ice. Stir well and garnish with a wedge of lime dropped in the drink.

—recipe courtesy of The Polo Lounge at The Beverly Hills Hotel in Beverly Hills, California

The Cocktail: White Russian

Description A scrumptious dessert drink and female favorite, although guys got more into this cocktail after "The Dude" in the film *The Big Lebowski* (1998) would imbibe nothing else.

Ingredients

2 oz. vodka   Milk or cream
1 oz. coffee liqueur

Directions Pour coffee liqueur and vodka in a rocks glass over ice and fill with milk or cream.

—recipe courtesy of The Fontana Lounge at The Belagio Hotel and Casino in Las Vegas, Nevada

THE MANLY DRINK YOU SHOULD TRY: BOURBON ON THE ROCKS

The big secret about whiskey is that it doesn't actually taste good, in the traditional sense of the word, to anyone. Think of it like a deep-tissue massage that hurts a little at first but eventually leaves you feeling nice and loose all over. Or put whiskey-drinking in the same category as driving a manual transmission—it may be more complicated and require more effort than an automatic, but it's a lot more interesting and involved.

"It's the flavors that are left on your tongue and the warm sensation in your gut that make whiskey enjoyable," says Parker Beam, master distiller at the Heaven Hill Distillery in Bardstown, Kentucky (his grandaddy's brother was Jim Beam himself). "It should have a smooth finish that lingers but never burns." Beam suggests pouring two ounces of a single barrel bourbon over ice in a rocks glass, and adding anything between a splash and two ounces of water depending on how strong you can take it. "Single barrel bourbon is the best for first-timers because it's held to the highest taste standards," says Beam. Most bourbons are made out of liquor from several different barrels, mixed together until the flavor comes out right—but single barrel bourbons have to taste perfect on their own.

5 things to know about whiskey/bourbon:

1. Bourbon is whiskey that contains at least 51% corn as the fermented grain, is no higher than 160 proof (that's 80% alcohol), and must be aged in unused, charred, white oak barrels (usually for six to eight years).

2. Kentucky whiskey has the same corn and proof requirements as bourbon, but it can be aged in previously used barrels (which changes the taste).

3. Tennessee sour mash whiskey is like bourbon, but it's put through a process involving sugar maple charcoal before being aged.

4. Any of the above can be "straight," which means not modified with neutral spirits, color additives, or flavor additives.

5. Any of the above can be "blended," which means neutral spirits, color additives, or flavor additives have been mixed in.

6. There's no right and wrong when it comes to which whiskey is best—it's all a matter of taste.

—information courtesy of www.oldwhiskeyriver.com

The Cocktail: Pink Lady

Description Order this pre-dinner drink when you're feeling dramatic—it was named after a Broadway musical that opened in 1911. It tastes mostly like a pomegranate.

Ingredients

1 ¾ oz. gin	1 egg white
1–2 dashes grenadine	⅔ oz. lemon juice

Directions Shake all ingredients with ice, strain into a martini glass, and garnish with a cherry.

—recipe courtesy of The Seasons Bar at The Four Seasons Hotel in Chicago, Illinois

JUNGLE LOOKS

What to Wear

Go glam: Upscale hotel lounges are the one of the few places where you can wear a Miss America style gown on a Tuesday night and not look overdressed (everyone will assume you've just come back from a charity ball).

Go corporate: Never underestimate the sex appeal of a woman in a suit—and fishnet stockings.

Go girlie: A final stronghold of good-old-boy sensibilities, a trip to a hotel bar is a great opportunity to indulge in old-fashioned femininity. Don a snug, fuzzy sweater and pencil skirt with a wide belt around your waist. To really revel in retro-chic, ask your mom to search through her closet for a pointy bra circa 1940.

JUNGLE TALES

Room Service Seduction

"My boyfriend and I were drinking in a hotel bar on a Friday after work when I spontaneously decided that we should stay the night. I told him I was going to the ladies' room, but instead I checked us into a suite and gave the bellboy a note sealed in an envelope that said 'Meet me in room 223. Love, Nina.' I gave him five bucks, pointed out my boyfriend, and told him to hand deliver it without a word. Then I dashed up to the room and stripped down to my bra and panties. When my boyfriend knocked on the door and I opened it half-naked, I swear his knees buckled. He grabbed me, slammed the door shut, and carried me to the bed. We got busy so many times that night we barely slept, but who cares!" —Nina, 30

The Cocktail: Lemon Drop Martini

Description In the mood to kiss? This super-sour martini will make you pucker up after every sip.

Ingredients

2 oz. citrus vodka	¼ oz. triple sec
2 oz. sweet and sour mix	Juice of 1 freshly squeezed lemon

Directions Shake all ingredients with ice and strain into a sugar-rimmed martini glass.

—recipe courtesy of The Polo Lounge at The Beverly Hills Hotel in Los Angeles, California

JUNGLE PARTY

Host a Casual Cocktail Night

Drink Menu

Four easy classic cocktails to offer are the Martini, the Gimlet, the White Russian, and the Champagne Cocktail. All together they only require four types of alcohol (vodka, gin, coffee liqueur, and bubbly) and they're different enough to satisfy disparate tastes. If you're running low on expendable income, ask friends to each bring a bottle of one type. That way all you'll have to provide is the vermouth, bitters, olives, lime juice, cream, and sugar.

Glassware and Garnish

You'll need three kinds of glasses and three kinds of garnish for this occasion: martini glasses, rocks glasses, and champagne flutes; and lemons, limes, and olives. Borrow the glassware from friends and neighbors a few days before to avoid having to buy. Same goes for cocktail shakers and jiggers.

Decorations

Throwing a cocktail party means celebrating an era when having a few friends over to mix martinis was a perfectly normal part of life, so as far as decorations go, all you need to do is clear away all visible clutter and dim the lights. The rest is alcohol. Set up a martini station in one corner of the room complete with glasses, gin and vodka, ice bucket, cocktail shaker and strainer, dry vermouth, a jar of olives, and jiggers for measuring. Let guests mix their own exactly the way they like them. For other drinks, set up bar in the kitchen so that the ice-filled freezer and sink are close at hand.

Audio and Visuals

Break out every jazz CD you have in the house, especially superstars like Thelonious Monk, Chet Baker, and John Coltrane. Play black and white films that feature lots and lots of cocktail drinking. Think *Casablanca* (1942), *Breakfast at Tiffany's* (1961), and *Notorious* (1946) (one of Hitchcock's lesser known suspense flicks that features a constantly sipping Ingrid Bergman).

COCKTAIL ASTROLOGY

What does your future hold? I'm not sure. But my crystal ball shows you holding a cocktail glass filled with a libation that's sure to enhance your aura.

Aries (March 21 to April 19)
Enthusiastic and passionate, you love to follow your heart—though it's quick to change its beat and send you off, yet again, to try something (or someone) new. You're a star socializer and have a knack for rallying people to get together and have a good time. Some people call you flighty, but that's only because you move so fast. Your cosmic cocktail: the Passion Fruit Martini—very of the moment.

Taurus (April 20 to May 20)
Your definition of the good life is a soft sweater, a delicious meal, and intimate, hushed conversation—sensual, comforting things. That's why you prefer lounges with couches to loud, chaotic clubs. Loyal and trustworthy, you're a gem of a friend. Your cosmic cocktail: the Mint Julep—perfect for sipping on porches.

Gemini (May 21 to June 21)
You've heard the twin thing a thousand times but that doesn't make it any less true. You really can see (and argue) both sides of every issue, and frequently feel two different ways about the same situation. You could call it contrary, but it also makes you breathtakingly broad-minded and dynamic—not to mention fun to talk to at a party. Your cosmic cocktail: the Strawberry Lemondrop—part sweet, part tart.

Cancer (June 22 to July 22)
Loving, affectionate, and sensitive, you give a lot of love to others and expect a lot in return. You also enjoy working on your pad, making it as cozy and luxurious as possible. A homebody, that's where you like to spend most of

your time, but everyone else is invited, too. Sometimes stubborn, it's your determination that makes you so successful. Your cosmic cocktail: the Chocolate Martini—comfort food in a glass.

Leo (July 23 to August 22)

The queen of the jungle, you radiate warmth and positive energy. Your magnetic personality makes you effortlessly popular and most people like you the moment they meet you. You can be opinionated, but that's only because you're usually right. You're great at encouraging friends to do and be their best— something you try to accomplish every day. Your cosmic cocktail: the Frozen Piña Colada—sunny, creative, and bold.

Virgo (August 23 to September 22)

Detail oriented and observant, you appreciate carefully made and delicate things—like a pearl button on a dress or a gourmet dessert. More than anything you love helping others, which makes your friends pretty damn lucky. On a bad day, you can be too critical, but your sharp eyes and mind make you an exceptional problem solver. You can figure anything out. Your cosmic cocktail: the Champagne Cocktail—feminine and refined.

Libra (September 23 to October 23)

Harmony should be your middle name because you're happiest when everyone is getting along. You hate fighting and will go to great lengths to avoid any kind of confrontation—which can make you evasive, but also easy to be with. That's a good thing, because you adore being with other people, especially your significant other. People love your ability to stay cool in stressful situations and always be fair. Your cosmic cocktail: the Long Island Iced Tea—equal parts rum, vodka, tequila, and gin.

Scorpio (October 24 to November 21)

You're sexy, scintillating, and downright dangerous when you want to be. Scorpios are great at getting what they want, usually because you can convince everyone else that that's what they want, too. Your insightfulness makes you a great advice giver, and your playful persuasiveness makes you an irresistible bedmate. Your cosmic cocktail: Bloody Mary—spicy!

Sagittarius (November 22 to December 21)

Philosophical and deep, you like to ponder the big questions in life and have a habit of letting your mind wander when it should be doing something useful. But your dreamy personality and brilliant mind attract a large number of fans who are hungry for your thoughtful point of view. You love bars and parties with creative themes. Your cosmic cocktail: the Frozen Zombie—it'll promote a total zone-out.

Capricorn (December 22 to January 19)

Practical and down-to-earth, you work hard and love to reap the rewards. You value simplicity and honesty and don't like complicated plans or fussy people. Friends adore your dry sense of humor, unwavering patience, and refreshing straightforwardness. Your cosmic cocktail: the Cape Cod—simple yet sensational.

Aquarius (January 20 to February 18)

Forward thinking and unconventional, you're so innovative, it can be hard for you to tolerate people who only think inside the box. You like to travel to unknown places, meet new people, and are always looking for ways to improve the world. People are drawn to your energy, optimism, and highly original ideas. Your cosmic cocktail: the Blue Margarita—very futuristic.

Pisces (February 19 to March 20)

Spiritual and mysterious, you're more mermaid than woman, and you might even be psychic. You live to use your imagination and you either do something artistic or at least appreciate other people's art very much. Guys love to drown in your eyes, and you have a calming effect on friends that keeps them coming back for more. Your cosmic cocktail: the Blue Fin—inspired by the sea.

The Tiki Bar

Every once in a while a party urge comes along that calls for more fun than you can have in reality. Maybe you just scored a new job, a new man, or a flirty little Hawaiian-print minidress that you're dying to wear even though it's December. Whatever the reason you're craving an over-the-top treat, nothing short of chugging rum out of a hairy coconut while surrounded by images of ancient Polynesian gods and exploding volcanoes is going to do the trick.

Tiki bars—the tackiest corner of the Cocktail Jungle—were invented to satisfy just this kind of urge. The disorienting effects of the garish decor are enough to give your brain a buzz, and the scrumptious cocktails are so smooth you won't notice the massive quantities of rum hidden within until you get up to go to the bathroom and the bamboo walls start spinning.

To fully enjoy the world of Tiki, it helps to know a little history. The first umbrella-worthy drinks appeared in 1934, when Earnest Beaumont-Gantt opened a bar called Don the Beachcomber in Hollywood and started whipping up dozens of rum-based tropical concoctions that tasted like they must have originated on remote island shores. In fact, Don was a native of New Orleans, and though he had been to Jamaica once or twice, he was using more imagination than experience to create one exotic recipe after another.

In 1944, Victor Bergeron, inventor of the hugely popular Mai Tai cocktail, opened a Polynesian-themed restaurant called Trader Vic's in Oakland, California. Suddenly Tiki bars were popping up all over the country and the trend was born. With the help of WWII vets looking to relive a little of the drinking and debauchery they indulged in while stationed in the tropics, island-themed films and books like *King Kong* (1933) and James Michener's Pulitzer prize winning book *Tales of the South Pacific* (1947), as well as the newly appointed statehood of Hawaii in 1959, Tiki culture remained a staple of every city's nightlife scene for almost three decades. The craze finally faded when '70s-style free love and psychedelic drugs made frou-frou drinks and paintings of topless maidens tame in comparison, but was revived in the '80s and '90s as a tongue-in-cheek way to celebrate the return of the cocktail. Now, in the first shaky years of the 21st century, Tiki is transforming back into a popular way to travel to an island paradise where pleasure is the first and only priority.

Ultimately a Tiki bar isn't suppose to be like any one place on earth, but rather a dizzying mix of tropical odds and ends that make you feel like you've completely escaped from everyday life. To that end, it makes perfect sense that Tiki drinks are usually a blend of several different fruit juices, liqueurs, and rums of all kinds. Piña Coladas, Bahama Mamas, and Rum Runners are the standards on every Tiki bar drink menu, but they're just the beginning. This chapter features recipes for those classics as well as more modern libations like a crisp Pineapple Martini and a completely updated Frozen Zombie. Garnished with tips on how to Hula dance, pick the perfect rum, and throw your own Bora-Bora bash, you've got all the knowledge you need to celebrate in genuine Tiki style.

The Cocktail: Hawaiian Punch

Description This classic recipe is a big hit at dance clubs in Honolulu because of its intense buzz-producing properties. It only takes one to make your inhibitions start to melt away.

Ingredients

½ oz. vodka
½ oz. peach-flavored bourbon
   (like Southern Comfort)
½ oz. sloe gin

½ oz. amaretto
1 oz. orange juice
1 oz. pineapple juice

Directions Build in a tall glass over ice cubes and stir.

—recipe courtesy of The Kahiki Lounge at Marion's Continental in New York, New York

The Cocktail: Frozen Zombie

Description Ice cold and pleasantly fruity, this totally new Zombie recipe is a dream to drink compared to the harsher-tasting classic yet still packs the same power.

Ingredients

2 oz. light rum

2 oz. dark rum

1 oz. pineapple juice

1 oz. orange juice

Splash of grenadine

1 tbsp. mango sorbet

¾ oz. 151-proof rum

Directions Blend all ingredients except 151 with a half-cup of crushed ice at low speed until slushy. Pour into a rocks glass then add a straw filled with 151-proof rum (to get the rum into the straw use a funnel or a squeeze bottle with a small spout), or simply float the 151 on top.

—recipe courtesy of The Zombie Hut in Brooklyn, New York

JUNGLE BASICS

The Rum Run-Down

Rum is a spirit made from the juice of the sugar cane plant. First the juice is boiled down to make molasses. Then the molasses is fermented and distilled to make rum. Some rums are distilled straight from the sugar cane juice without the extra step in between.

Rum's image is all about lounging on the beach during the day and indulging in adults-only pleasures at night. Sugar cane is grown in tropical climates, notably the islands of the Caribbean and West Indies, so it's only natural that rum has become associated with vacation, sun, and sin.

Types of rum include light, dark, fruit-infused, and spiced. Light rum is watery in texture and has a strong alcohol flavor—it's what most bartenders reach for when someone orders a rum and Coke®. Dark rums have more flavor and go down smoother. The difference is in the fermentation process. The longer the rum is fermented, the thicker and sweeter it is. Rums that are really dark or "black" have added caramel coloring which deepens the shade but doesn't affect the taste.

In general, substituting an older rum for a younger one will improve the taste of any drink. Using a spiced variety like Captain Morgan's Spiced Rum can lace any cocktail with a hint of cinnamon, nutmeg, and ginger (particularly great in daiquiris). Malibu Caribbean Rum is the most widely used flavored rum and has an extremely sweet, coconut flavor.

Citrus-flavored rums like Bacardi Limón and Bacardi O (orange) deliver a refreshing tang and are great for martinis. Many brands make a 151-proof rum which contains about twice the alcohol of the average bottle. To make any Tiki drink more dangerous, float a half-ounce of 151 on top after pouring. Two interesting rums to keep an eye out for are Bacardi Ciclón, a blend of 90% rum and 10% tequila, and Cabana Boy flavored rums (there's raspberry, pineapple coconut, citrus, wild cherry, and vanilla spice) which feature a photo of a shirtless hunk on every bottle. The best rum to buy someone as a gift? $40 Mount Gay Extra Old from Barbados. It's a blend of 7-, 8- and 10-year-old rums that connoisseurs swear by.

The Cocktail: Grapefruit Daiquiri

Description This was Ernest Hemingway's favorite drink at the Floridita Bar in Old Havana, Cuba. It's tart and refreshing—perfect for when you're working up a sweat doing the Hula.

Ingredients

1 oz. fresh-squeezed lime juice

1 oz. cane sugar syrup (or 1 tsp. sugar)

3 oz. fresh-squeezed grapefruit juice

3 oz. anejo rum

Directions Blend all ingredients with a cup of crushed ice until smooth (add 3 or 4 chunks of fresh grapefruit for more flavor).

—recipe courtesy of The Mai-Kai in Fort Lauderdale, Florida

The Cocktail: Frozen Rum Runner

Description This gem of a recipe is for the one-and-only original Rumrunner created in 1972 at The Tiki Bar on Holiday Isle. The blackberry and banana liqueurs soothe your taste buds as the undercurrent of rum slowly carries you away.

Ingredients

½ oz. premium rum	⅛ oz. banana liqueur
½ oz. 151-proof rum	⅝ oz. grenadine
⅛ oz. blackberry brandy	1 oz. lime juice

Directions Blend ingredients on low speed with a cup of crushed ice and serve in a tall glass.

— recipe courtesy of The World Famous Tiki Bar at Holiday Isle in Islamorada, Florida

MATING CALLS

Start a Conversation in a Tiki Bar

Ice Breaker #1: Order a drink that features flames, hold it up to a handsome stranger, and invite him to make a wish and help you blow it out.

Ice Breaker #2: Ask the cutie next to you at the bar if he knows what's in a Mai Tai. He won't, but now you can ask the bartender together.

Ice Breaker #3: Break out some Brady/Tiki trivia: When the Brady boys find a bad luck Tiki in Hawaii (Episodes 73, 74, and 75), what three horrible things happen? What was the name of crazy Professor Whitehead's (played by Vincent Price) beloved Tiki that he talked to as if it were alive?

Ice Breaker #4: With the cooperation of a few friends, send a foxy guy a fancy tropical drink via a waitress. Have her tell him that it's from the girl who has two umbrellas in her cocktail. He'll eyeball everyone's drink until his gaze lands on you and your crew whose glasses all feature double parasols. What man wouldn't come over and investigate?

Ice Breaker #5: Wear a coconut bra and watch the boys come to you.

WHO IS TIKI?

According to Polynesian mythology, Tiki is the first man
ever created. In the 1950 nonfiction adventure classic
Kon-Tiki, ballsy zoologist Thor Heyerdahl—a real-life
Indiana Jones—writes of an old man he meets on one
of the Marquesas islands in 1937, who says "Tiki . . .
was both god and chief. It was Tiki who brought my
ancestors to these islands where we live now.
Before that we lived in a big country beyond the sea."

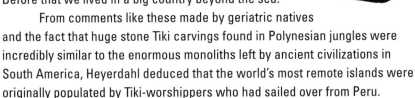

From comments like these made by geriatric natives
and the fact that huge stone Tiki carvings found in Polynesian jungles were
incredibly similar to the enormous monoliths left by ancient civilizations in
South America, Heyerdahl deduced that the world's most remote islands were
originally populated by Tiki-worshippers who had sailed over from Peru.

The theory was tossed out because scientists thought it was ridiculous
to assume that anyone could survive such a long, harrowing trip on the primitive
vessels used at the time. To prove that such a journey was possible, Heyerdahl
and a few colleagues built a balsa wood raft similar to those made by early
Peruvians and made the trip themselves, surviving by the
skin of their teeth. When the book and documentary film of the same
title hit the scene, Heyerdahl's fellow Norwegians weren't overly
impressed, but Americans went wild for the story and the documentary ended up winning an Oscar. Of course, all the attention on the
original Tiki made Tiki bars and restaurants even more popular.

The term Tiki now refers to any primitive-looking carving
that depicts a Polynesian supernatural power, or is used like
"disco" or "grunge" to describe an entire fad and all its associated objects, music, style, attitude, and atmosphere. For more
dirt on all things Tiki, check out Sven Kirsten's coffee-table-
worthy *Book of Tiki.*

The Cocktail: Polynesian Iceberg

Description This is a mild and yummy drink for anyone who wants to start the night off slow and happens to love bananas. The phallic garnish is a great conversation piece.

Ingredients

2 oz. banana liqueur

1 oz. orange juice

1 oz. pineapple juice

1 small banana

Directions Puree half of the small banana then add remaining ingredients and blend with ½ cup crushed ice. Use the other half of the banana as garnish.

—recipe courtesy of The Tiki Room in New York, New York

The Cocktail: Bahama Mama

Description A simple recipe for this Spring Break classic, the rum mixed with cream of coconut recalls an afternoon in Nassau spent smearing suntan lotion on a hot frat boy.

Ingredients

2 ½ oz. dark rum

1 oz. cream of coconut

Splash of orange juice

Splash of pineapple juice

½ oz. grenadine

Directions Shake all ingredients except for grenadine with ½ cup crushed ice and pour into a rocks glass. Top with a grenadine floater.

—recipe courtesy of The Tahiti Restaurant and Tiki Lounge in Los Angeles, California

FIELD GUIDE TO GUYS

Species: The Gay-Seeming Straight Guy

Common Physical Traits: Stylish pants, a trendy shirt, two earrings, product-

enhanced hair, a Gucci watch, neatly plucked eyebrows, slim, yet buff, bod
Scent: Designer bath products and Gucci Rush
Animal Behavior: Wittily chatting up everyone at the bar, spreading juicy
celeb gossip, and sizing up women based on their clothes.
Natural Habitat: The Tiki Bar
Tips for the Gay-Seeming Straight Guy Hunter: Wear something big,
eye-catching, and trendy—like a fur tank top. He won't be able to resist
coming over and commenting on it.
What You'll Get for Your Birthday: A Diane Von Furstenberg wrap dress

JUNGLE SOUNDS

Tiki Tracks

These tunes are frequently heard drifting
from the speakers of a Tiki bar like a warm
ocean breeze.

Esquivel *Space Age Bachelor Pad Music*
(Bar/None, 1994)
Vegas bandleader Juan Garcia Esquivel perfected
his silly style of whacked-out pop in the late '50s and
early '60s (think the *I Dream of Jeannie* theme song).
Trombones, slide guitars, and lyrics like "Boink boink! Shame,
fuddy fuddy" are sure to put you in a tipsy, far-out state of mind.

Mondo Exotica (EMD/Capitol Records, 1996)
This CD is part of Capitol Records' Ultra Lounge series and is packed with
bubbly and creamy tunes that are meant to recall a night spent on an unexplored
island—from a mellow sunset to a savage cannibal attack. An ideal intro to
the bizarre musical genre of "exotica."

Martin Denny *The Exotic Sounds of Martin Denny* (EMD/Capitol)
Martin Denny is the person famous for bringing "exotica" (a.k.a. mysterious music that's designed to transport you to a funky, faraway place) into the mainstream. This is a two-CD set that will fill your apartment with sexy voodoo love songs.

Kenny Sasaki & The Tiki Boys *Tiki Moon* (www.kensasaki.com, 2002)
Japanese composer and bassist Kenny Sasaki has mixed jazz, reggae, Latin, Hawaiian, Polynesian, and rock to create a modern instrumental Tiki lounge soundtrack that goes down incredibly smooth.

Arthur Lyman *Taboo* (RYKO, 1958)
Lyman played the vibraphone in Martin Denny's band then went off on his own to mastermind hushed jungle music with hypnotic percussion and the occasional animal call. Pop this in your stereo to create an atmosphere of lush, green vegetation, hanging vines, and countless pairs of eyes glowing from behind the bushes.

The Cocktail: Frozen Piña Colada

Description Creamy and dreamy, this cocktail is the diva of Tiki drinks. Real pineapple and coconut milk infuse it with the true taste of a beach side vacation.

Ingredients

⅓ cup chopped pineapple	¼ cup coconut milk
2 ½ oz. coconut- or pineapple-flavored rum	1 tsp. fresh lime juice
	1 tbsp. sugar

Directions Blend ingredients with a cup of crushed ice and pour into a cocktail glass.

—recipe courtesy of The Tahiti Restaurant and Tiki Lounge in Los Angeles, California

The Cocktail: Piña Colada Quickie

Description When you have a craving for a Piña Colada but don't have time to chop pineapple or deal with a blender, this lighter, fizzier version is ideal.

Ingredients

2 oz. coconut-flavored rum

Splash of pineapple liqueur

Splash of pineapple juice

Soda water

Directions Pour rum over ice into a rocks glass. Add pineapple liqueur and pineapple juice then fill the rest of the glass with soda water.

—recipe courtesy of Politiki in Washington, DC

JUNGLE MOVES

Be a Hula Bombshell

Angie, Helen, and Tara Pontini, a.k.a. The World Famous Pontini Sisters, get paid to raise hula all over the country—from the Tiki Bar at The Venetian Casino in Las Vegas to The Kahiki Lounge at Marion's Continental in New York. Here are four of the fabulous dance trio's favorite Hawaiian moves. Angie says any chick who knows how to swing her hips can pull them off; just put a gentle smile on your face and think about the rhythm of rolling waves, the wind blowing through the trees, and fish swimming in the sea.

The Little Fisher Girl

Softly march in place by lifting your feet just half an inch off the ground with every step, as if you're climbing a miniature set of stairs. Use your hips! Now swing both of your arms up over your left shoulder and then slowly pull them diagonally across your body. The idea is that you're pulling a fishing net over your left shoulder and casting it away into the ocean so that your hands land down by your right hip. Repeat this fluid motion a few times and then cast the net from over your right shoulder.

The Polynesian Princess
Step onto your left foot and plant it flat on the floor, swinging your left hip out to the side. Then point your right foot out in front of your left foot. Now step right and plant your right foot on the floor, swinging your right hip to the side, then point your left foot out in front of your right one. Repeat these two steps while holding your arms up to the sides with elbows out and your hands on the top of your head, imitating a leafy crown.

The Hoochy Lau
Stand with your feet shoulder-width apart, legs slightly bent, and start rolling your hips from side to side in classic Hula-girl style. Hold your hands out to the side with softly bent elbows and keep your hands palms-up as if balancing drinks on them. Isolate your hips as much as possible and try not to move your upper body. Occasionally take tiny steps forwards and backwards and/or cross your arms in front of your chest and then bring them back out to the sides. Gently roll your fingers, simulating a breeze blowing over the tops of the waves your hips are creating.

The Holy Hula
Using your hips to enhance every motion, take a tiny step to the right with your right foot and then take a tiny step out to the left with your left foot. Then step to the right with your right foot again and now bring your left foot over and touch the ground lightly about an inch away from the inside of your right foot, then bring it back to the left. Now bring your right foot over and lightly touch the ground about an inch away from the inside of your left foot and then bring it back out to the right. Repeat: step right, step left, step touch, step touch. Your knees should be slightly bent, giving the illusion that your hips are moving

more than they really are. While doing the step, cross your hands in front of your heart so that your thumbs are hooked together and your fingers are fluttering out to the sides like a butterfly.

The Cocktail: Kokomo

Description It's the surprising addition of vanilla schnapps that makes this concoction especially yummy. Serve it up after dinner as a liquid dessert.

Ingredients

2 oz. coconut rum	3 oz. pineapple juice
1 oz. dark rum	1 oz. orange juice
1 oz. vanilla schnapps	Splash of grenadine

Directions Shake all ingredients and pour over ice in a tall glass.

—recipe courtesy of The Tiki Bar on Solomon's Island, Maryland

JUNGLE LOOKS

What to Wear When It's Tiki Time

Date-Night Tiki: For a romantic rendezvous opt for a sundress or miniskirt by designers like Lily Pulitzer and Shoshanna who combine tastefully playful prints with drop-dead sexy shapes. Choose a slinky tank in a matching solid color to top off bottoms that are just a little bit loud. Strappy, high-heeled sandals or floral flip-flops add the finishing touch.

Minimal Tiki: If "subtle" is the best word to describe your style, wear all black, sweep your hair into a bun, and secure a single hibiscus bloom at the base of it as your only accessory.

Maximum Tiki: Backyard bash? Bachelorette party? Beach side bonfire? Wear the official Hula-girl get-up. At www.surfwearhawaii.com you can get a grass skirt, bikini top, floral lei, and book of Hula tips for around $17.

JUNGLE TALES

Drunken Insanitiki

"One night my best friend and I were drinking piña coladas at a beach side bar in the Bahamas when two cute guys wearing all-white (turns out they were sailors on a millionaire's yacht) dared us to go skinny-dipping with them. We said 'what the hell' and followed them down to the water. By the time we got there, they were already naked and running into the surf. Just as we were about to strip down and join them we both caught sight of an enormous leaping jaguar that was tattooed across one of the sailor's rear ends. It was a skinny-dipping deal breaker. We laughed hysterically, grabbed their clothes, and dropped them in front of the open-air bar so they'd have to flash everyone in order to get them back. We were zipping away in a cab just as we saw them walking buck-naked up the beach."—Kelly, 28

The Cocktail: Suffering Bastard

Description Did your boyfriend or husband have a rough day? Make him feel better with a cocktail designed to soothe a man's worst woes.

Ingredients

2 oz. tequila

2 oz. sloe gin

2 oz. cranberry juice

2 oz. pineapple juice

Squeeze of lime

Directions Build over ice in a tall glass.

—recipe courtesy of The Kahiki Lounge at Marion's Continental in New York, New York

The Cocktail: Freak My Tiki

Description A complex-tasting club elixir that gets you good and ready for a night of dancing, this is one of those unforgettable drinks that make you forget everything.

Ingredients

3 oz. melon-flavored vodka

1 oz. peach schnapps

1 oz. cranberry juice

Splash of fresh lime juice

Directions Shake all ingredients with ice and then strain into a martini glass.

—recipe courtesy of The Tiki Room in New York, New York

THE MANLY DRINK YOU SHOULD TRY: DARK AND STORMY

This island favorite is like Enrique Iglesias in a glass—rich, spicy, and seductive. Use dark aged rum and authentic Caribbean ginger beer (don't confuse it with its milder cousin ginger ale) for the sultriest results. To make: pour 1 oz. dark rum and 4 oz. ginger beer over ice in a highball glass.

JUNGLE PARTY

Throw a Tiki Bash

Drink Menu

The easiest way to serve up tropical cocktails to a roomful of friends is to pick just four drinks and create a little photocopied drink menu complete with images of Tikis, volcanoes, coconuts, Hula girls, gorillas, etc. for your guests to peruse. That way you can practice just those four recipes until you make them fast and delicious every time. School at least two of your closest pals on how to make them too, in case someone's glass empties when you're deep in conversation or busy powdering your nose. Be sure to include at least one frozen drink in the mix and one classic favorite.

Glassware and Garnish

Though a martini glass is mandatory when called for, 12 oz. ceramic Tiki mugs and 8 oz. genuine coconut cups are the core of any Tiki party. Tiki bowls are also ideal when serving couples (most bowls have a spot in the middle where you can pour a shot of 151 and set it on fire). Garnish your drinks with one or more of the following: an orange slice, half a pineapple wheel, a cherry. Add a swizzle stick and paper umbrella or fake flower for that over-the-top look that's truly Tiki.

Decorations

One of the easiest ways to prep your pad for a Tiki bash is to go to a fabric store and purchase several yards of a Hawaiian print fabric that's as pretty or tacky as you like. Use it to cover tables, make temporary slipcovers for furniture, and hang it from doorways to create curtains. A few raffia table skirts are a great touch, as are wooden Tiki statues scattered about and Tiki masks on the walls. To create an instant Tiki bar, cover a table with straw matting and let the matting hang down to the floor on the side that faces the room. Give the bar and other tables a pretty border by cutting flower leis and attaching them end to end around the tabletop's edge (or use floral garlands to do the same). Floral borders also work around large pictures, windows, and the TV. Display a vase filled with real orchids, hibiscus, or red ginger in a central place or put individual flowers in bud vases and place them on windowsills. In the bathroom, remove the shower curtain and fill the tub with water. Then tint it with blue curacao and set plastic or real flowers and floating candles adrift. Some party stores sell large fake leaves that look great on top of tables or hanging from the walls. It's pretty much impossible to decorate too much. The best tip is to keep plastic to a minimum so that your party has all the true textures of an island paradise.

Lighting

For outdoor soirees, bamboo torches recreate a dangerous, romantic mood that leads to spontaneous makeout sessions. Indoors, string lights that feature palm trees, Tikis, flowers, or jungle animals will give off a pleasantly low glow. If none of your friends is a pyromaniac, lots of candles can create the fiery thing inside.

Audio and Visuals

Fill your CD changer with the albums featured in this chapter and play island-themed movies with the sound turned down for background eye-candy. A few great DVDs to choose from: *King Kong* (1933), *South Pacific* (1958), *Blue Hawaii* (1961), *Blue Lagoon* (1980), and *Cast Away* (2000).

You can get all the Tiki supplies mentioned here on these cyber spots:

www.tikibosko.com

www.tikitrader.com

www.tikifarm.com

www.tropictreasures.com

www.munktiki.com

Glossary

THE FIELD GUIDE TO GLASSES

Stock up on these seven essential glasses and you can serve up just about anything. Haven't you heard that guys make passes at girls with the right glasses?

Martini Glass
The elegant triangular glass with the slim stem—it isn't just for martinis anymore. Dreamed up during the Bauhaus design craze of the 1920s, it gives drama to any cocktail that isn't served with ice.

Rocks Glass (a.k.a. Old Fashioned or Whiskey Glass)
This short, stout glass holds four to eight ounces and is used to serve up any number of on-the-rocks or frozen cocktails as well as whiskey straight-up. The best rocks glasses are a little bit heavy, so that even if your drink is small in quantity it feels substantial in your hand.

Highball Glass
Taller and slimmer than a rocks glass, a highball holds eight to twelve ounces and can be used to hold everything from its namesake cocktail to other classics like a gin and tonic or screwdriver.

Shot Glass
These little guys have a dual purpose. First and foremost, they're used to get 1 ½ or 2 ounces of straight booze down your throat in a hurry. But they're also a good measuring tool (just make sure you know exactly how much your shot glass holds).

The Pint Glass

It's what most bars serve draft beers in because it's less cumbersome than a beer mug or a pilsner glass. And when you're not partying, these make the best everyday water/soda glasses.

Champagne Flute (a.k.a. Tulip Glass)

If you simply can't bear to serve champagne in anything else but this delicate four to ten ounce glass, there's no getting around keeping a few in your cabinet. The skinny tulip shape helps keep the carbonation from escaping too fast. Unfortunately, they're not good for anything but bubbly and champagne cocktails.

All-Purpose Wineglass

White wineglasses are smaller than red wineglasses because it's better to keep the white chilling in the bottle than sitting in your glass for too long. Red wineglasses are larger and have a rounder, more balloon-like shape. Your best bet is to choose a medium-sized, slightly rounded glass that will work perfectly well for both.

JUNGLE SURVIVAL GEAR

You can't make a cocktail without the right tools. Here are the basics:
Blender (make sure it's strong enough to crush ice)
Bottle Opener
Citrus Stripper
Corkscrew
Cutting Board
Strainer
Jigger (for fast mixing, get one in each size: ½ oz., 1 oz., 1 ½ oz., and 2 oz.)
Measuring Cup
Measuring Spoons
Mixing Glass (a pint glass will do)
Muddler (a thick wooden pestle used to crush ingredients in a glass)
Pitcher (for water or margaritas)
Cocktail Shaker and Strainer
Long Spoons (for stirring)

JUNGLE JARGON

A Mini-Guide to Cocktail Talk
Bitters A spirit infused with powerfully bitter or bittersweet herbs. Bitters are used to flavor cocktails, and usually just a splash is enough.
Chill To chill a martini glass, fill it with ice and set it aside while you mix the cocktail in a cocktail shaker. Dump the ice out of the glass before pouring in the drink.
Float A layer of liquor that sits on top of the drink. To create a float, hold a spoon over the glass, and slowly trickle the ingredient over the back of the spoon so that it falls gently on the surface of the drink.
Frost To frost a glass, run it under cold water, then put it in the freezer for twenty minutes.

Grenadine A strong, sweet, red syrup made from pomegranates.

Muddle To crush ingredients like fruits and herbs to extract their juices or oils. This is usually done with a "muddler."

Simple Syrup (a.k.a. sugar syrup) A mixture of water and sugar used in many cocktails. To make simple syrup, put equal parts water and sugar in a bottle of any size and shake. Store in the fridge and use whenever a recipe calls for it.

Shake Place ice, followed by ingredients, into a cocktail shaker and combine ingredients by vigorously shaking it up and down.

Stir A cocktail is stirred rather than shaken to blend ingredients lightly and to avoid making the drink cloudy. Cocktails should only be stirred ten to fifteen times.

Strain European cocktail shakers come with built-in strainers. American cocktail shakers don't, requiring that you buy one separately.

Vermouth This wine infused with herbs and other ingredients is most frequently used to make a vodka or gin martini. Dry vermouth contains 5% sugar. Sweet vermouth contains 15% sugar. An open bottle of vermouth will go bad in about two weeks. Store it in the refrigerator to make it last longer. You know it's time for a new bottle when, like stale wine, it starts to smell a little like vinegar.

FIELD NOTES

_____

_____

_____

_____

_____

_____

_____

_____

_____

_____

_____

_____

_____

_____

_____

_____

_____

_____

_____

FIELD NOTES

FIELD NOTES